CONTE

ACKNOWLEDGEMENT AND DEDICATION

The job of collecting many of the facts and figures used in this book would have been made very much harder without the stacks of stats already gathered in one place at the superb *England Football Online* website: www.englandfootballonline.com

So, by way of a thank you, this book is dedicated to the website's compilers:

Josh Benn, Alan Brook, Chris Goodwin and Peter Young

Make sure you pay their website a visit, readers. It's almost as amazing as this book!

Stop writing!

There always comes a time when a writer has to stop writing and hand his book over to the publisher to start publishing. In the case of *England!* that date was 31 December 2005. Since then, of course, England have unhelpfully played more football matches and messed up a few of my facts (such as how many matches England have played in their history!). So if you do happen to spot a mistake, it might not really be a mistake, just a slightly-out-of-date fact which will be updated when I write the next edition – until the time comes to stop writing...

Michael Coleman

INTRODUCTION

Well over 1,000 footballers have played for England since the first international match against Scotland in 1872 – although the earliest players would find things have changed a lot since their day...

In this book you'll read all about the history of the England football team, from that first-ever game in 1872 right up to the present day.

You'll read about some of the amazing characters who've been lucky enough to pull on the England shirt. Like...

- The striker who became a lion.
- The player who kept his shirt but gave away his shorts.
- England's most-injured captain.

The book is organized into sections based on the different managers England have had. Like the teams they picked, some of these managers were frightfully good – and some were just frightful! Such as...

- The manager who couldn't even get his team in the changing room.
- The manager accused of picking turnips.
- The manager who said he wasn't good enough to be manager.

And, as if that isn't enough, watch out for the winners of our acclaimed *Foul Football* awards as well. Awards such as...

THE HIGHEST AWARD POSSIBLE FOR MATCH BALL DELIVERY
Switzerland v. England, 1938

Because a visit from the England team was so special, the Swiss match organizers decided that having the referee carry out the match ball was too boring. They had it dropped on to the pitch from a low-flying aeroplane instead!

So read on. And if you find the facts and stories exhilarating but the jokes a bit excruciating, don't worry. Tell yourself it's just like watching England!

AMATEUR ASSORTMENTS (1870–1914)

Before 1870, the only football matches in England were played between club sides. These clubs had names like The Old Etonians and The Old Harrovians. Why? Because their players had all been to the same school. (Etonians went to Eton and Harrovians went to – no, not Harrov, but Harrow. They weren't very hot on spelling.) These players were amateurs; that is, they didn't get paid to play. They played for love, not money – just like when you play for your school football team!

HE SAID WE CAN USE HIS BALL FOR THREE DOUGHNUTS AND A SHERBET DAB!

Then, in 1870, a different kind of match was organized: an *international* match between England and Scotland! Imagine you're a top club player. How do you think you'd have been chosen to play in this match?

a) You were spotted by a talent scout.

b) You answered an advert in a newspaper.

c) You were recommended by your club.

Answer: b) The advert appeared in a London newspaper called *The Sportsman* and asked for any footballer who wanted to play in the match to send in their details!

9

The advert had been placed by members of the English Football Association (FA for short), who'd decided it would be a good idea to organize the first-ever international football match. So they picked the date, the ground, and – from the replies they got to their advert – both teams!

It was mostly London-based players who were picked, of course, because only they would have seen the advert! The FA had a way round that problem. If the players who put themselves forward were English they played for England, and if they had some Scottish connection – either they were born there or they had a Scottish granny – then they qualified for the "Scotland" team!

WHAT'S YOUR CONNECTION WITH SCOTLAND?

WELL, I ONCE ATE A WHOLE HAGGIS...

The game was played on 5 March 1870. Because of the way both teams were chosen, neither this match, nor the four similarly organized matches that followed it in 1870–1871, are regarded as "proper" internationals.

FIVE FA FACTS

1 The English Football Association was formed in 1863. It is the oldest FA in the world.

2 The FA is in charge of all football played in England, from top professional matches down to school games!

3 Any team that wants to play in a proper competition has to be "affiliated" to the FA.

4 Anybody involved with an affiliated team, such as a manager or a chairman – or a headteacher! – can be chosen to be a member of one of the FA's committees.

5 From 1888 until 1963, one of these committees was known as "the international selection committee". Its job was to pick the England team!

The first "real" international between England and Scotland took place in 1872, on 30 November. To show that the FA knew that places outside London existed, they'd agreed to play at the West of Scotland Cricket Ground in Glasgow. But the most important difference was that for this match both England and Scotland picked their own teams. England chose theirs from the 100 or so football clubs playing by then. Scotland's problem, with only 10 clubs in the whole country, was rather harder. They ended up picking the whole side from their best club, Queen's Park – but at least they *had* picked it. What's more, Queen's Park were no mugs … they held England to a 0–0 draw!

Even without any goals, the match was seen to have been a great success. One newspaper, the *North British Mail*, reported (rather grandly):

The game established a record, as it was played in the presence of the largest assemblage previously seen at any football match in Scotland, close on four thousand – including a number of ladies – being present.

Another, called *Bell's Life*, enthused:

> Altogether it was one of the jolliest, one of the most spirited and pleasant matches that have ever been played.

After this, the FA changed their approach to finding the best players. If you'd wanted to be picked for the next game against Scotland, in 1873, you'd have had to be recommended by your club – and no less than 70 players were! You'd then have been put into a team called "Probables" or "Possibles" and been watched as you played in a trial match.

At the end of all this activity, the selection committee would have sat down and picked the team. It sounds a long-winded business, but it worked. England won the 1873 match, beating Scotland 4–2.

Cap that!

You've been picked for England! So, what do you have as a memento? At an FA meeting on 30 January 1886, the assistant secretary, N.L. Jackson, came up with the answer. Heading wasn't part of the game at that time, and footballers wore different coloured caps along with the rest of their kit. So what Jackson suggested was that:

> *All players taking part in future England internationals be presented with a white silk cap with a red rose embroidered on the front. These to be termed "International Caps".*

After four months' discussion, the FA decided they preferred royal blue to white and that the date of the game should be on the peak, but apart from that the idea was accepted. Other changes were made as years went by, with the name of the opposing country being added to the peak, a pretty silver tassel sewn to the top and the English rose replaced by the same three lively lions (signifying bravery) found on the Queen's flag.

Awarding international caps must been a good idea, though, because it's lasted until now. Players are *still* given real caps when they play for England – even if they only get on as substitute for 20 seconds!

England all-stars: James "Pretty" Prinsep

James Prinsep won his first and only England cap in 1879. He played half-back (nowadays he'd be called a midfielder) for a team called Clapham Rovers. One newspaper writer claimed that James was: "One of the prettiest half-backs who ever did duty."

By "pretty", he didn't mean gorgeous but "skilful". Another writer said he was: "Always very cool, very strong on his legs; kicks splendidly."

MASHER'S PLAYING VERY PRETTILY TODAY

PRETTY VIOLENT!

Not bad for a 17 year-old! Yes, when "Pretty" Prinsep ran out at the Kennington Oval on 5 April 1879 for England's match against Scotland (just a week after playing on the losing side with Clapham Rovers in the FA Cup Final), he was only 17 years and 245 days old.

James Prinsep won a couple of other medals that no modern player is likely to match, though. As he was an amateur, football was really Prinsep's hobby. The job he was paid to do was to be a soldier.

His army career took him to Egypt. While serving there he was twice given medals for jumping in to save people from drowning in the River Nile!

Proud professionals

By the middle of the 1880s, professional footballers had arrived – that is, footballers whose clubs paid them to play for them. The amateur organizers at the FA didn't like professionals. They thought that a player who earned extra if his team won couldn't possibly play as fairly as an amateur. So, even though professionals were soon playing for England alongside amateurs, the two certainly weren't regarded as equal...

Question: Imagine that you're a professional footballer in 1885. What are you expected to call any amateur player in your team?

Answer: a) Yes, the low-down professional had to show his respect for the squeaky-clean amateur by calling him "Sir" – which must have produced some strange-sounding shouts during a match...

Nineteen-year-old James Forrest of Blackburn Rovers was the first professional to play for England against Scotland, in 1885 – in spite of Scotland's objections. They wanted internationals to be kept strictly amateur. It's not known whether poor young Forrest objected to having to call the other ten players in the team "Sir", but he'd have had good reason.

The amateurs' lack of trust in professionals playing football in the right sporting spirit even found its way into the rules of the game. The FA, whose job it was to keep the rules of football up-to-date, invented a special offence. What was it called?

a) Unsporting behaviour.

b) Ungentlemanly conduct.

c) Professional fouling.

In spite of all this, the number of professionals grew. By 1891 England was fielding a wholly professional team. That doesn't mean that the professionals had taken over, though – because England fielded a wholly amateur team, too! On 7 March 1891, while an England amateur team was beating Wales 4–1, an England professional team was beating Northern Ireland 6–1. Insultingly for the Welsh and Irish, the FA had told all the English players involved that the games were being treated as trial matches to select the team to play Scotland!

THE PROVE-THE-AMATEURS-WERE-RIGHT-ALL-ALONG AWARD...

Steve McMahon, England (1988–1990) who said: "I'd kick my own brother if necessary. That's what being a professional is all about."

YOUNGEST PLAYERS

James Prinsep's record as the youngest England player stood for over 125 years – until it was broken by a certain Wayne Rooney. Here are the facts about England's five most baby-faced boot-wearers:

1. Wayne Rooney (Everton) v. Australia, 12 Feb 2003
Age: 17 yrs 111 days
2. James Prinsep (Clapham Rovers) v. Scotland, 5 Apr 1879
age: 17 yrs 253 days
3. Thurston Rostron (Darwen) v. Wales 26 Feb 1881
Age: 17 yrs 312 days
4. Clement Mitchell (Upton Park) v. Wales, 15 Mar 1880
Age: 18 yrs 24 days
5. Michael Owen (Liverpool) v. Chile, 11 Feb 1998
Age: 18 yrs 59 days

COMMITTEE CONCOCTIONS (1919–1939)

Between 1914 and 1918, the First World War put a stop to international matches. So it wasn't until 1919 that (another) FA committee sat down to think about who it might be a good idea for England to play. In the previous 50 years, England had spent most of its time playing Wales, Scotland and Northern Ireland in their own little British Championship. It was getting boring. Wales were too easy to beat (28 wins out of 36 games, even when using a reserve team) and Northern Ireland even easier (28 wins out of 33). Scotland were a lot harder (only 13 wins out of 43), but one interesting match a year wasn't enough. By now, football had spread all over the world. There was a far wider choice of countries for England to beat!

They'd tried a European tour in 1908. It had been a great success, with England beating Austria twice (6–1 and 11–1), Hungary (7–0) and Bohemia (4–0). So in 1921 England hopped across to Belgium, winning 2–0. Two years later, in 1923, the countries played a return match, with Belgium becoming the first foreign country to play an international on English soil. Poor Belgium went home badly soiled themselves; England beat them 6–1!

England all-stars: Charles Buchan

Charles Buchan, of Sunderland and Arsenal, played only six internationals. His debut was in 1913, and it wasn't a happy one. It was against Northern Ireland, in Belfast – and the Irish won, 2–1, to beat England for the first time. After the match, Buchan heard one of the linesmen criticize his performance. Not surprisingly, he gave him an earful in return – only to discover that the linesman was also an England selector!

Belligerent Buchan missed a few games after that, but was picked again for England's away match in Belgium in 1921, when he scored one of England's two goals. Unfortunately for him, in that match he offended the selectors yet again by displaying what they thought was ungentlemanly conduct. What did he do?

a) He shook somebody's hand.
b) He gave away a penalty.
c) He challenged the Belgian goalkeeper.

Answer: c) He put his foot in the way as the Belgian goalkeeper kicked the ball out. It hit the sole of his boot, then hit the bar. Challenging a goalkeeper simply wasn't done outside England, and the crowd howled at Buchan for the rest of the game – which the FA chaps found awfully embarrassing.
a) Shaking hands, *wasn't* ungentlemanly conduct –

---

but, amazingly, it wasn't thought to be *gentlemanly* conduct either, as Buchan soon found out. Proving what an unpredictable lot the selectors were, Buchan was not only picked for England's next tour match, in France in 1923, he was made captain! So, when England took a 1–0 lead, he felt as captain that it would be good for team spirit if he ran across and shook the scorer's hand. Oops! Chastened Charles was severely told off for it afterwards. As far as the FA selectors were concerned, shaking hands was far too wild a celebration!

Pick 'n' mix

It's generally thought that Charles Buchan would have played more games for England if he hadn't annoyed so many selectors. They were in charge, and what they said counted. By the 1920s, all the England players were professionals – but the England selectors weren't. They were mostly chairmen of Football League clubs who'd made pots of money doing something like being a butcher. Being in charge of a football club was their hobby. It was a serious hobby, though. They all wanted the honour of having their players turn out for England. So it's been claimed that meetings to select England's team often went rather like this:

As you'll discover, this remained the way of doing things for another 40-odd years. Ray Wilson, England's left-back from 1960 to 1968, was one of the players who thought it was a mad system. He said:

You had people who wouldn't know a ball from a tomato picking the side. They'd choose players they'd seen having a good day.

Ingenious excuses

By 1929, England had lost a good few games against Scotland, Wales and Ireland. Those results had been bad, but not a disaster.

Occasionally, though, somebody was brave enough to suggest that the other team's players might have been better. Bob Crompton, who captained England 22 times in 41 appearances between 1902 and 1914, was such a man. He once said:

The Scots are more intelligent, more skilful and have better use of the ball. If they were as fast as they were clever, England would have little chance with them.

When England began losing matches against foreign teams, though, then it became a far more serious matter. There simply *had* to be a reason why England had been beaten...

- On 29 May 1929, Spain became the first foreign side to beat England when they won 4–3. *English excuse: It was too hot for football.*

The newspaper *Athletic News* complained:

Beads of perspiration were dropping off the chins of our players as they ran about.

• In 1936, England played away to Austria, a team coached by a man named Willy Meisl. Austria won 2–1. *English excuse: The players had done too much walking before the match.*

This might have been true! On the morning of the match, Meisl had kindly offered to show England's players the sights of Vienna, Austria's capital. The players accepted his offer – only to find themselves on more of a marathon march than the short stroll they'd expected. Maybe Meisl's first name should have been "wily" not Willy!

• This attitude lasted some time. In 1948 England would travel to little Switzerland and lose 1–0 after a terrible performance. *Future English excuse: The players had been given too much to eat by their Swiss hosts.*

A newspaper report would claim:

> The only possible explanation is that our boys were sluggish from a too-sudden immersion in an ocean of food.

Back in the 1930s, though, England were usually good enough not to need an excuse. The World Cup had started in 1930, but the FA hadn't wanted England to take part. Why not? For the simple reason that they *knew* England were the best, so what was the point of travelling to some tournament to show it?

The team proved them right, too. Italy, winners of the World Cup in 1934, came to England and were beaten 3–2. Four years later, in 1938, Germany were the hot favourites to win the World Cup. Then *they* ran into England…

Germany and England weren't the best of friends in 1938. Adolf Hitler had just sent his troops to invade Austria and everybody was worried that war wasn't far away. This was what happened when England played in Berlin:

• The whole stadium was a sea of waving German swastika flags – except for one little corner…

• Where two lonely England fans were holding two tiny Union flags.

• The England team lined up for the national anthems. They'd been told that, when the German anthem began, they had to keep Adolf 'appy by giving the straight-arm Nazi salute.

• The players weren't at all pleased about this, but they did it – as they looked straight at those two little Union flags.

• When the game finally began, though, they didn't have to worry about keeping Adolf 'appy at all. They were free to make him unbelievably *unhappy*!

• England scored. The Germans equalized. Then England scored two more!

• With a minute of the first half to go, England's star winger Stanley Matthews dribbled round three defenders and banged the ball into the net to make it 4–1!

• Half-time was tough. The England players found

themselves climbing towards the sky! England had been given a changing room at the very top of the stadium and had to climb 90 tiring steps to reach it.

• But were they tired? No! They scored another goal, while Germany scored two. It was now 5–3 ... and time for one of the best goals ever seen in an international! Here's how it went:

• Stanley Matthews ran down the wing, then crossed the ball high into the middle of the pitch.

• In raced Len Goulden of West Ham United, winning one of his 14 England caps. Without waiting for the ball to bounce, goalden Goulden hit it on the volley from about 22 metres out... and sent it rocketing into the goal so hard the net was knocked off the hooks holding it to the crossbar!

• Final score: 6–3 to England!

THE 'GET-YOUR-OWN-BACK' LOUDEST-SCREECH AWARD

Len Goulden, England (1937–1939) ... who, after smacking in his wonder goal against Germany celebrated by yelling at the top of his voice:

Let 'em salute that one!

Germany, their confidence shattered by the defeat, went to the 1938 World Cup and were quickly knocked out.

England's record from 1872

From the first international to the end of the 1939, this was England's record with teams picked by the FA's selection committee:

Played	Won	Drawn	Lost	Goals For	Goals Ag
226	138	37	51	674	293

None of those matches involved either the World Cup or the European Championships. As we've seen, the FA were too snooty to enter England for the World Cup. Nobody could say they were too snooty to enter the European Championships, though – but only because the competition hadn't yet been invented!

That was all in the future...

THE BRITISH CHAMPIONSHIP

The British Championship – or "Home International" Championship, to give the competition its first name – was completed 88 times between the 1883–1884 and 1983–1984 seasons. It wasn't played during either the First or the Second World War, nor in 1980–81 when bombs were going off in Ireland.

It was a league competition, with the four countries playing each other once. Goal difference and stuff like that didn't count until 1979 – if countries were level on points then they shared the title.

England excelled, as you'll see from the Home Championship facts.

	Won outright	Shared	Total titles
England	34	20	54
Scotland	24	17	41
Wales	7	5	12
Ireland*	3	5	8

*just Northern Ireland from season 1921–1922

THE CAPTAINS COURAGEOUS QUIZ

Since the wonderfully-named Cuthbert J. Ottoway of Oxford University led the team out for their first international in 1872, over 100 players have had the honour of being named captain of England. Test your knowledge about ten of them!

1 Stan Cullis captained England just once, in 1939. Without a team manager, the captain was expected to sort out arguments over tactics. What complaint did inside-forward Raich Carter come to him with about winger Stanley Matthews?

2 Even captains have to start somewhere. Johnny Haynes captained England 22 times between 1960 and 1962, but his first nervous international was against Wales in 1957. After an experienced Tom Finney had guided him through the match, Haynes offered to repay the favour in any way he wanted. What did Finney suggest?

3 One of Terry Butcher's seven appearances as England's captain was against Sweden in 1989. At the end of the match his shirt was covered in – what?

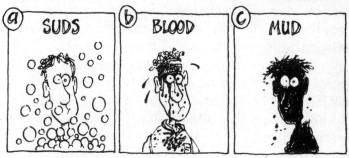

4 Bobby Moore captained England 90 times, but nearly missed No. 64. Why?
a) He'd been arrested.
b) He'd been kidnapped.
c) He'd been lost.

5 David Platt captained England 19 times, the first against San Marino in 1993 ... a game in which he scored four in a 6–0 win! What did he do with the shirt he wore that day?

a) He framed it.

b) He swapped it for the San Marino goalkeeper's jersey.

c) He gave it to his old school.

6 Alan Shearer was put on trial for his first three games (of an eventual 34) as captain. What did he have to do to continue?

a) Help out his defence.

b) Score as many goals as usual.

c) Smile more.

7 Tony Adams captained England 15 times – although everybody knew he couldn't remember England's famous World Cup win in 1966. Why not?

a) He didn't like football.

b) He wasn't English at the time.

c) He hadn't been born.

8 Not all captains get on well with their managers. Gary Lineker captained England 18 times under manager Graham Taylor. But what did Taylor say about him after he'd missed a penalty in a 1–1 home draw against Brazil in 1992?

a) "We only played with ten men."

b) "We could do with a penalty-taker who can kick straight."

c) "We need a new captain."

9 Very occasionally, captains are appointed as a reward. Pony-tailed goalkeeper David Seaman's single appearance as captain came on his 50th international appearance. TV pundit and ex-manager Brian Clough wasn't impressed. What did he say about dapper David?

a) "He couldn't catch a cold in the Arctic Circle."

b) "You can't keep goal with hair like that."

c) "My 90-year-old gran can jump higher than he can."

10 In 2003, during England's 2–1 win over Serbia and Montenegro, captain Michael Owen was substituted. The captain's armband then passed (via a dunk in the mud) to Emile Heskey, Jamie Carragher and Phil Neville as further substitutions took place. How many captains did England have that day?

a) 4 **b)** 1 **c)** 0

Answers:

1a) To which Cullis replied, "Don't worry about it. Just run into the penalty area and wait for it to arrive there."

2c) Finney ran a plumbing business alongside his football. He told Haynes he could do with some help to put in a bathroom because his labourer had gone sick!

3b) The appropriately-named Butcher had sustained a cut to his head that later needed ten stitches.

4a) In Colombia, before travelling to Mexico for the 1970 World Cup, Moore was arrested after being accused of stealing a bracelet. He was finally released to play a great part in the tournament – and the accusers were eventually jailed for lying.

5a) Platt's pongy shirt went into its frame complete with captain's armband – unwashed!

6b) Manager Glenn Hoddle thought the responsibility of being captain might affect Shearer's goalscoring. But sharp-shooting Shearer scored three goals in his three-game trial and kept the job!

7c) Adams was the first player to be picked for England who'd been born after the 1966 World Cup.

THE MOST LITERATE CAPTAIN AWARD...

Tony Adams, England's captain during Euro 2000, who revealed that during the tournament he'd been reading William Shakespeare's *Henry V* – which contains Henry's famous speeches before going into battle!

8a) Taylor's suggestion that Lineker wasn't there didn't stop him picking him as captain for quite a few more games – until famously substituting him in his final game when Lineker was one goal short of the England scoring record.

9b) Clough added, "That Seaman is a handsome young man but he spends too much time looking in his mirror, rather than at the ball."

IT MAY NOT LOOK GOOD BUT IT HAS ITS USES!

10b) The official match records only show the player who starts the match as captain; the others are regarded as no more than arm-band carriers!

WALTER'S WOBBLERS (1946–1962)

Eighteen months after their famous football match in Berlin, England and Germany were fighting each other in the Second World War. Football carried on, through friendly games and wartime leagues. Wartime internationals were played, too, but caps weren't awarded for these matches.

By the time England played their next proper international, against Northern Ireland in September 1946, there had been many changes to the team.

Question: How many of the 1938 team against Germany continued to play for England after the war?
a) Fewer than 2 **b)** 2 to 4 **c)** More than 4

Answer: a) Just one – the amazing Stanley Matthews of Stoke City and Blackpool. He won the first of his 54 caps in 1935, aged 19 ... and the last in 1957, at the ripe old age of 42!

There was another change, too. For the first time in their history, the England team had a full-time manager. For the ten years or so before the war, what had happened was:
1 The FA selection committee picked the team.
2 They invited a different club manager to travel with the team for each match and make suggestions about tactics – which meant they were given different suggestions every game. So, not surprisingly...

36

3 The players went out on the pitch and did what they felt like.

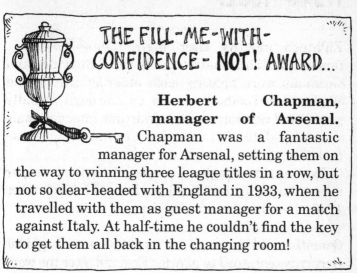

THE FILL-ME-WITH-
CONFIDENCE - **NOT**! AWARD...

Herbert   Chapman, manager   of   Arsenal. Chapman was a fantastic manager for Arsenal, setting them on the way to winning three league titles in a row, but not so clear-headed with England in 1933, when he travelled with them as guest manager for a match against Italy. At half-time he couldn't find the key to get them all back in the changing room!

This first-ever England manager's name was Walter Winterbottom. He'd played just a couple of games in Manchester United's defence before a back injury had forced him to give up and turn to teaching PE. He'd done this so well, and had so many bright ideas about playing football, that the English FA offered him a brand-new job. But what exactly did he do as manager?

Question: Which of these tasks is the odd one out – the one Walter *didn't* do?
a) Organize coaching.
b) Pick the team.
c) Give newspaper interviews.
d) Do the cooking.

> **Answer: b)** Yes, during his time as England manager, wonderful Walter did everything *except* pick the England team!

The FA saw his main job as being England's Director of Coaching – not only the coaching of the top stars, but right down to schoolboy level. He'd also be the man who answered the questions of newspaper reporters both before and after England matches.

> ## THE HEAD COOK AND BOTTLE-WASHER AWARD...
>
> **Walter Winterbottom.** When the England team travelled to Brazil for the 1950 World Cup, the food in their hotel was so awful that WW took over in the kitchen and cooked it himself!

But pick the team? No, that was still the job of the FA's international selection committee. Admittedly Walter *was* a member of the committee and *was* able to say who he'd like them to pick – but he was often outvoted!

Walters's woes

• Winterbottom later complained, "The selection committee saw an England cap as a reward for loyal service. There was no attempt to build a team."

• Nobody could argue with that. During Walter's time in charge, no fewer than 160 different players turned out for England – 34 of them only once.

• Sometimes the players hardly knew each other. In 1955, a friendly against Denmark was arranged for the Sunday after a full league programme the day before. Obviously, those picked for the international couldn't turn out for their clubs – so, to try and be fair, the selectors chose a team with one player from each of eleven different clubs!

• Being a top man didn't guarantee your place either. In May 1960, Bill Slater of Wolverhampton Wanderers learned that he'd been dropped from the team. The same day he also learned that he'd been voted *Footballer of the Year*! It didn't do him any good. He was never picked for England again.

Whether Walter picked the team or not, England had some fantastic early wins during his reign as manager.

In 1947 England played in Portugal ... eventually. Before the game began there was an argument about – what?
a) The size of the pitch.
b) The size of the ball.
c) The size of Portugal's goalkeeper.

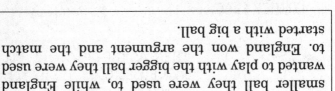

Answer: b) Portugal wanted to play with the smaller ball they were used to, while England wanted to play with the bigger ball they were used to. England won the argument and the match started with a big ball.

Twenty seconds later it was in the Portugal net – England had scored to make it 1–0!

Another twenty seconds later, Portugal were kicking off to restart the game – but with a small ball. After being picked out of the net, the English one had been whacked into touch and quickly swapped for the Portuguese ball!

It didn't help. By half-time England were 5–0 ahead and so much in control that Stan Mortensen, scorer of four goals that day, ran across to the Portugal bench and suggested they throw the first ball back on as well to give their team something to play with!

England finished the match 10–0 winners. As for Portugal, they were so embarrassed they couldn't face turning up for the traditional after-match banquet. They stayed away and had a good bawl!

The legend of Stanley's comb

A year later, in 1948, England secured a famous win in Italy. The Italians were the reigning world champions and England beat them 4–0. It was during this match that winger Stanley Matthews did something that became talked about all round the world. Try it in your next school match:

DRIBBLE THE BALL DOWN THE WING AS FAR AS THE CORNER FLAG;

THEN, AS THE OPPOSING FULL BACK EDGES CLOSE TO TACKLE YOU...

PULL OUT A COMB FROM YOUR SHORTS: USE IT TO TIDY YOUR HAIR: THEN PUT IT BACK IN YOUR SHORTS AND DRIBBLE ROUND THE FULLBACK!

Wherever smart Stan went in the world, people would come up to him and tell him it was the most amazing thing they'd ever seen happen during a game. Once, on a visit to South Africa, he was even greeted by hordes of children waving a mixture of flags ... and combs!

There was only one thing wrong with the story: it wasn't true. The match had been played on a swelteringly hot day and Matthews had done no more than wipe his hand on his shorts, then brush his

41

sweaty hair out of his eyes. But it had looked to some of the crowd as if he'd taken something out of his pocket (shorts had pockets in 1948).

So the legend had been born. You could say it was a case of "hair today – but not gone tomorrow"!

MISERABLE MATCHES
ENGLAND V USA
1950

Thursday 29 June, 1950 was the day that Walter's Wonders became Walter's Wobblers.

Twenty years late, England had finally entered the World Cup. The finals were held in Brazil. England flew in to newspaper headlines, which announced: "The Kings of Football have arrived!"

Question: England's first match was against Chile. How did they prepare?
a) By watching films.
b) By sending a spy to watch them play.
c) By reading glossy magazines.

Answer: c) "All we knew about South American teams," said Tom Finney, "was what we'd read in magazines"!

After beating Chile 2–0, England travelled to Belo Horizonte to meet the USA. This is how the game went, by numbers.
1 England attack.
2 They repeat step 1 for 37 minutes.

3 USA score a fluke goal. A wild shot bounces of the head of USA's Joe Gaetjens and goes into the England net.

4 England attack.

5 They repeat step 4 for the rest of the game except when the ball goes into the crowd filled with USA fans and is passed around to waste time!

During the match, England hit the woodwork three times and the USA's goalkeeper Frank Borghi made loads of miraculous saves, especially one right near the end from a free kick taken by Tottenham defender Alf Ramsey (remember this name!).

England had lost 0–1. When the score appeared in the newspapers next day, everybody thought it was a misprint and should have read 10–1!

THE CATCH-US-IF-YOU-CAN AWARD...

Frank Borghi, USA. America's goalkeeper only played football for fun. His main sport was baseball!

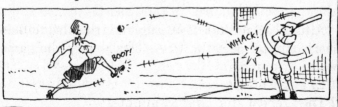

England all-stars: Nat Lofthouse

Nathaniel ("Nat") Lofthouse won 33 caps between 1950 and 1958. In those games he scored a thrilling 30 goals. He was a powerfully built player and if there was any tough stuff happening on the pitch then it was a fair bet that Nat would be in the middle of it...

• When England travelled to South America in the spring of 1953, Nat nearly caused a riot during a match against Chile. One of his shots hit a Chilean player smack in the face. When he collapsed, a gang of his team-mates tried to make Lofthouse collapse as well – by attacking him. Then the crowd joined in by hurling oranges. Nat had the last laugh, though: he scored the winner to give England a 2–1 victory.

NAT GRABBED ONE GOAL AND FORTY-THREE ORANGES

• In May 1955, England drew 1–1 away to Spain in another rough match. In this one, Lofthouse ended the first half as naked Nat, after his shirt had almost been ripped off by a Spanish defender. The team didn't carry lots of spare shirts in those days, so Nat had to play the second half without a number on his back.

• Nat was pretty nippy, though, and he never showed this to better effect than against Austria in Vienna, in the same month. With the game at 2–2, Lofthouse was just inside the Austrian half when he ran on to a long throw from England's goalkeeper, Gil Merrick. This is what happened next (<u>Health Warning</u>: do NOT try this during a match unless you're wearing a crash helmet and a full set of body armour)…

LOFTHOUSE WAS ELBOWED
IN THE FACE… BUT NAT
KEPT GOING…

AUSTRIA'S RIGHT BACK
RACED OVER TO CHALLENGE
HIM… BUT NAT KEPT GOING…

BLOOD WAS NOW STREAMING
DOWN HIS FACE… BUT
NAT KEPT GOING…

THE AUSTRIAN GOALKEEPER
RACED OUT TOWARDS HIM…
BUT NAT KEPT GOING…

HE JUST MANAGED TO TOE POKE
THE BALL PAST THE KEEPER AND STOPPED.
THIS TIME IT WAS THE KEEPER WHO KEPT
ON GOING, RIGHT INTO NAT…

MOMENTS LATER,
NAT WAS FLAT…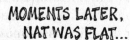

BUT THE BALL KEPT ON GOING…
STRAIGHT INTO THE GOAL TO
GIVE ENGLAND A 3-2 WIN!

Nat was carried off on a stretcher, only to bravely reappear for the last five minutes of the game – long enough for him to hit the post and just miss out on a hat-trick.

Question: After this performance, Lofthouse was given a nickname that stayed with him for the rest of his career. What was it?

a) Lion Lofthouse.
b) Lofthouse the Leopard.
c) Leaping Lofthouse.

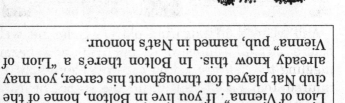

Answer: a) Nat Lofthouse was nicknamed "The Lion of Vienna". If you live in Bolton, home of the club Nat played for throughout his career, you may already know this. In Bolton there's a "Lion of Vienna" pub, named in Nat's honour.

MISERABLE MATCHES
ENGLAND v HUNGARY
1953

For 30 years, ever since Belgium had sailed over in 1923, England had managed to hang on to one proud record: they'd never been beaten at home by a foreign side. All that changed on 5 November, 1953. That day, in a dazzling display of footballing fireworks, England's record went up in flames!

Here's how the newspaper reporters saw things – before, during and after this historic match.

46

Before:

This Hungarian team is no better than the one England beat 6-2 in 1936.

It will be a pushover.

England should finish two or three goals to the good.

And when the Hungarian players came out well before kick-off (unheard of in 1953) and began juggling the ball around on the Wembley pitch, an injured Tom Finney, sitting in the stand, heard a reporter say:

They might be able to do that now, but they won't be able to do it when the game starts!

During:

Unfortunately for England, Hungary did *exactly* that when the game started! England were 0–1 down after 45 seconds and losing 2–4 at half-time. Hungary's third goal had been scored by their captain, Ferenc Puskas, who'd completely fooled England's captain Billy Wright by skilfully dragging the ball away from him with the sole of his boot, changed feet and rifled the ball past Merrick. *The Times* said:

Billy Wright rushed into the tackle like a fireman racing to the wrong fire.

Hungary went on to win the match 6–3. Ex-England player Charles Buchan, by now a reporter with the *News Chronicle*, didn't mess about:

We were outplayed, outgeneralled, outpaced and outshot.

In other words, England's defeat was an out-and-out disaster!

After:

Yesterday the inevitable happened. England at last were beaten by the foreign invader.

Now it's back to school for England.

The lesson is clear. Our best is not good enough nowadays.

THE BIG BOOT AWARD...

Shared by Alf Ramsey, Bill Eckersely, Harry Johnston, Ernie Taylor, Stan Mortensen and George Robb. All six played against Hungary that day – and all six never played for England again.

THE MOST-STUPID-HEADLINE-WRITING AWARD...

The *Daily Mail*. Six months later, before England played the return match in Hungary, the newspaper carried the bold headline: "England Chance of Revenge – Hungary Worried". Hungary's only worry was about keeping count as the goals flew in; they belted England 7–1!

Walter's wilderness timeline

The rest of Walter Winterbottom's time in charge of the England team was a bit of a wilderness period.

1958 Tragedy strikes. The plane carrying the Manchester United team home from a European Cup match crashes at Munich airport. England players Duncan Edwards, Tommy Taylor, Roger Byrne and David Pegg are all killed.

1959 After failing to get out of their group in the 1958 World Cup finals in Sweden, England go on a tour of South America. They're beaten by Brazil, Mexico and, worst of all, whacked 4–1 by little Peru. For the first time, the newspapers begin calling for a new manager.

1961 England suddenly hit form, scoring 40 goals in six matches, including a 9–3 win over Scotland!

1962 Unfortunately, the good form doesn't last until the 1962 World Cup in Chile. England just about survive their group (losing to Hungary, beating Argentina and drawing with Bulgaria), only to be knocked out in the quarter-finals by Brazil.

In 1962, England's team was built round their captain and No. 10, Fulham's Johnny Haynes. Asked about his tactics before meeting England in their 1962 World Cup group match, Baroti, the Yugoslav coach said: "10 takes corners, 10 takes throw-ins, 10 does everything. What do we do? We put a man on 10. Goodbye England." It worked. Haynes hardly had a kick of the ball and Hungary won 2–1.

For the first time, England's lack of success was being blamed on their manager. Walter's family noticed it, too. Nobody would speak to Mrs Winterbottom in her local supermarket. His son was teased at school. Walter decided that it was time to go.

Walter Winterbottom's last game in charge of England was a 4–0 victory over Wales on 21 November 1962. Afterwards, the players gave him a set of drinking glasses as a present. In 1978 the Queen made him *Sir* Walter Winterbottom.

England's record under Walter Winterbottom

Played	Won	Drawn	Lost	Goals For	Goals Ag
159	78	55	28	383	196

ENGLAND FACT FILE

AROUND THE WORLD

England's entry into the 1950 World Cup began the serious business of football globetrotting that has grown steadily ever since. Some of the countries they've played don't exist any more – and other countries are popping up all the time. Here are the facts!

First five foreign opponents*

1 Austria	6 Jun 1908	England won 6–1
2 Hungary	10 Jun 1908	England won 7–0
3 Bohemia	13 Jun 1908	England won 4–0
4 Belgium	21 May 1921	England won 2–0
5 France	10 May 1923	England won 4–1

Newest five foreign opponents*

1 Slovakia	12 Oct 2002	England won 2–1
2 Macedonia FYR	16 Oct 2002	England drew 2–2
3 Liechtenstein	29 Mar 2003	England won 2–0
4 Serbia Montenegro	3 Jun 2003	England won 2–1
5 Azerbaijan	13 Oct 2004	England won 1–0

*Scotland, Wales, Ireland and Northern Ireland don't count as foreign!

ALF'S ACES
(1963–1973)

The next England manager
was Alf Ramsey.
(Remember him? He was in the team when England
famously lost to the USA in 1950. He was also one of
the players who was never picked again after the 6–3
belting by Hungary.)

After finishing his career with Tottenham Hotspur,
Ramsey had gone on to manage little Ipswich Town of
the third division ... and amazed everybody by
turning them into League Champions. Impressed by
this, the FA offered Alf the job of England's manager.
He accepted – on one condition...

Yes, Alf Ramsey's condition for becoming England
manager was that he alone would pick the team.

Champions!

After Ramsey's first game in charge, a horrible 2–5 defeat by France, he boldly proclaimed:

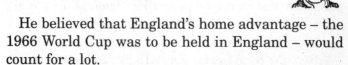

England will win the World Cup in 1966.

He believed that England's home advantage – the 1966 World Cup was to be held in England – would count for a lot.

Before the tournament, England used friendly internationals to try something completely new: playing with no wingers. As well as defending, the poor old full-backs were expected to charge up and support the forwards as well. Sometimes they could manage it, and sometimes they couldn't. When they couldn't, England looked really boring. This caused the newspapers to give England a nickname. What was it?

a) Ramsey's robots.
b) Ramsey's rumblers.
c) Ramsey's rabble.

But England were growing in confidence. When the time for the tournament came around, nothing was left to chance. For instance, to guard against any chance of the players injuring themselves or doing something that would lead to a septic toe, they were given lessons on how to cut their toenails!

☆ MAGIC MATCHES ☆
ENGLAND V WEST GERMANY
1966

On 30 July 1966, England reached the World Cup Final, just as artful Alf had said they would. The story of that day is well known – but here's what happened, with a few extra things you might not know...

• For almost two hours before the match begins, massed bands play 16 tunes – one for each country in the finals.

• Germany kick off to start the 200th ever World Cup game.

•Germany score through Helmut Haller.

• England equalize – in a move started by the referee! After whistling for a free kick, Gottfried Dienst kicks the ball to England captain Bobby Moore, who places it then passes to Geoff Hurst, who scores with a header.

• During half-time the band show who they're supporting. They play the "Colonel Bogey"

march – a tune whistled by British soldiers when they marched off to war with Germany!

 •It suddenly pours with rain ... but the clouds are lifting for England.

 •England go 2–1 up through a goal scored by Martin Peters.

 • Defender Jack Charlton tries to waste some time by passing back to goalkeeper Gordon Banks – but England's fans boo him, yelling, "We want three!"

 • The fans are stunned into silence as Germany scramble an equalizing goal to make it 2–2.

 • England kick off – and the referee blows his whistle. It's time for extra time. Alf Ramsey comes on to the pitch to tell his team: "You've won the World Cup once – now go out and do it again."

 • Geoff Hurst hits a shot against the German crossbar. The BBC commentator Kenneth Wolstenholme shows what a load of tosh commentators sometimes talk as he babbles:

> *Yes! Yes! No! No! The linesman says no! The linesman says no! It's a goal! It's a goal! Oh and the Germans go mad at the referee.*

Thankfully, everybody watching could see that the linesman had supported England's claim that the ball had bounced down over the line. England were 3–2 up.

• Half-time in extra time. Alf Ramsey comes on to talk to his players again ... and tidies up as well, by carrying off a bag of oranges that somebody's left on the pitch.

• The same Kenneth Wolstenholme of the BBC proves that sometimes commentators don't talk tosh by uttering three of the most famous sentences ever:

There are people on the pitch. They think it's all over.

And, as Hurst smashed in his third goal to make it 4–2 for England:

It is now!

• England have won the World Cup. Jack Charlton falls to his knees; brother Bobby bursts into tears. Ramsey's Robots are about to be given a new nickname: The Wingless Wonders!

THE PROUDEST MUM AWARD...

Florence Ramsey. Manager Alf's 71-year-old mum had been too nervous to go to the match, so she'd watched it at home on the telly. Afterwards she said of her son, "He's been saying for three years that England would win the World Cup. Now that his prophecy has come true, I am the proudest mother in Britain!"

England all-stars: The team of '66 ... and their medals

Have you ever won a medal for anything? A football cup-winners' medal, for example? If not, imagine you have. What would you do with it? Put it on a shelf and polish it every day – or throw it under your bed to gather dust?

When the members of England's team left Wembley after their match against Germany, they all had precious World Cup winners' medals safely tucked away in their bags. Here's what happened to the Team of '66 ... and those famous medals.

Gordon Banks (1963–1972, 73 caps): In his playing days, Gordon's goalkeeping was so safe he was nicknamed "The Banks of England". His England career came to a sad end in 1972 when he lost the sight in one eye after a car crash. He sold his medal in an auction in 2001.

George Cohen (1964–1967, 37 caps): A solid right-back, George belongs to a World Cup winning family. His nephew, Ben Cohen, was in the England team that won the Rugby Union World Cup in 2003! Ben's still got his medal, but George hasn't. It's now on display in the trophy room of the only club he ever played for – Fulham.

Ray Wilson (1960–1968, 63 caps): Elegant left-back. Wilson (his real first name was Ramon) retired at the age of 34 after getting a bad injury. He left football altogether and went into his family business – as an undertaker! Did he bury his medal? No, he sold it to an unknown buyer.

THE DON'T-KNOW-WHICH-WAY-TO-TURN AWARD...

Ray Wilson, who, knowing that after his injury he'd never be as good a player again, said seriously, "I knew I'd be going backwards and I wasn't looking forward to that..."

THIS WAY   THAT WAY

Nobby Stiles (1965–1970, 28 caps): A terrier half-back, Stiles (his real first name was Norbert) was a little bloke with a crunching tackle. In his autobiography he revealed that during the World Cup he went to church every morning at 7 a.m. Perhaps he's since been praying that he won't need the money and have to sell his medal, because he's still sticking close to it – just like he did with opposing forwards!

GROWL!

Jack Charlton (1965–1970, 35 caps): The lanky central defender was nicknamed "The Giraffe". After retiring, he became a manager, taking the Republic of Ireland to a couple of World Cup finals tournaments. Asked where his World Cup winners' medal was, he once shrugged and said, "In a drawer somewhere". It must still be there because he's since said he'd never, ever sell it.

Bobby Moore (1962–1973, 108 caps): England's captain. The great Brazilian, Pele, said that Moore was the best defender he ever played against. Sadly, brilliant Bobby died in 1993, at the early age of 51. His widow sold his medal and lots of other stuff to Bobby's old club, West Ham United, to display in their museum.

Alan Ball (1965–1975, 72 caps): A midfield dynamo who was always on the move, Ball did much the same after he finished playing, by becoming manager of lots of different clubs. He sold his World Cup winners' medal in 2005, saying: "Winning the World Cup in 1966 will stay with me for ever, but it's time to look to the future, not the past." It wasn't a bad-looking future, either – action-man Alan's medal sold for £140,000!

Bobby Charlton (1958–1970, 106 caps): When the hotshot forward/midfielder stopped playing, he decided he'd try to teach youngsters how to do it and began the famous Bobby Charlton Soccer Schools. The school's most famous pupil? A certain David Beckham, who became skills champion for his age group when he was eleven years old! Although Bobby still owns his World Cup medal, it's always on display in his old club, Manchester United.

THE PLAY-IT-SAFE AWARD...
Bobby Charlton, whose house was burgled in 2003 by crooks hoping to steal his World Cup medal ... but by then he'd already given it to Manchester to keep safe in their safe!

Geoff Hurst (1966–1972, 49 caps): Hat-trick hero striker Hurst was only winning his eighth cap when he played in the World Cup final. He didn't realize he had become an overnight celebrity until he went to the supermarket with his wife and everybody wanted his autograph! A former West Ham player, his winners' medal sits alongside Bobby Moore's in the West Ham club museum.

Martin Peters (1966–1974, 72 caps): Midfield man Peters, who scored England's second goal in the Final, has still got his medal. You can bet it's insured, though – because when he retired from playing he set up an insurance business!

Roger Hunt (1962–1969, 34 caps): Striker Hunt is best known for a goal he didn't score – the Hurst shot in the final that came down from the bar. Instead of charging at the ball to force it into the net, Hunt turned away to celebrate. England supporters insist that this was proof it went over the line. Germans say it only proves that Hunt's eyesight was dodgy! At least he doesn't have far to look for his medal. He's another of the Team of '66 who's still got it.

Player problems

England's time at the top lasted four years – until the next World Cup in Mexico, 1970. Along the way, they had a few player problems…

• In 1968, during a 0–1 defeat against Yugoslavia, midfielder Alan Mullery became the first-ever England player to be sent off. England's proud record of never having a player sent off in an international had come to an end – after 424 matches and 89 minutes!

• In 1969, World Cup winner Roger Hunt said he didn't want to play for England again. The newspapers were running a campaign to bring Jimmy Greaves (dropped in favour of Geoff Hurst in 1966) back into the team. Ramsey left Hunt out, but...

THE I-DON'T-DO-WHAT-YOU WANT AWARD...

Alf Ramsey, who showed the newspapers what he thought of their campaign ... by never picking Greaves again!

• After winning his third cap in a tour match in Mexico in 1969, another player, Everton's goalkeeper Gordon West, also said he didn't want to play for England again because trips abroad didn't agree with him. What did West always suffer from?
a) Homesickness
b) Nerves
c) Stomach bugs

THIS MAN NEEDS PLENTY OF FRESH AIR... HE SHOULD TAKE UP A SPORT

Answer: a)

There were plenty of other players who did want to turn out for England, though, and everybody thought the team was good enough to win the 1970 World Cup as well. Unfortunately, they weren't. West Germany gained revenge for 1966 by knocking England out in the quarter-finals, winning 3–2 in extra time after being two goals down.

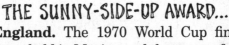

THE SUNNY-SIDE-UP AWARD...

England. The 1970 World Cup finals were held in Mexico, and there were fears that the players might stay out in the sun too long. So they were rationed to just 30 minutes of sunbathing. Halfway through, trainer Harold Sheperdson would blow a whistle for "turn over". When his second whistle came, 15 minutes later, the players knew it meant, "You're done!"

YOU CAN'T BE TOO CAREFUL

High(land) jinks

Although by the 1970s many internationals had become qualifying matches for the World Cup and European Championships, England were still playing friendly internationals. Except that, when they were against Scotland, they weren't so friendly...

• In 1967, Jack Charlton got a broken toe and Ray Wilson a whacked ankle as England were beaten 2–3 at Wembley. Scotland immediately called themselves the new World Champions!

• In 1972 the two countries celebrated the 100th anniversary of their first "proper" international encounter in 1872. It was a game that started with a bang. After just 30 minutes there'd been one goal (to England) ... and 46 free kicks! Things only got better after the referee called the two captains together and told them to calm things down.

• The following year, 1973, saw another pair of 100th celebrations. Bobby Moore won his 100th cap, and Scotland's own FA were celebrating their centenary. At the end of the match, though, only England were smiling. They'd just won the game 5–0!

 **THE I-DO-LOVE-SCOTS-REALLY AWARD...**

Joe Baker, of England (1959–1966, 8 caps) ... and Scotland. Baker had been born in England but moved to Scotland when he was just six weeks old. As a result, he spoke with a broad Scottish accent. This meant that everybody booed Baker – England fans because of his accent and Scots fans because he played for England!

MISERABLE MATCHES
ENGLAND V POLAND
1973

England needed to win this game to qualify for the 1974 World Cup finals. A draw wasn't good enough – that would put Poland through.

Straight from the kick-off, England went on the attack. And stayed on the attack for almost the whole 90 minutes. In that time they clocked up a massive 35 attempts on goal – of which Poland's goalkeeper, Jan Tomaszewski, used his hands and knees and elbows to save 34. With not much of the match left to play, the only shot that had beaten him had been a penalty, scored by England striker Allan Clarke.

Up at the other end, how many shots had Poland managed on England's goal? A measly 2! The trouble was, one of them had gone in!

So, with just a couple of minutes to go, the score was 1–1. Would England score the vital winner? What they needed now was a super-sub…

"Get ready, Kevin!" yelled manager Alf Ramsey at the substitute's bench.

Kevin Keegan didn't need to be told twice. He leapt to his feet and began pulling off his tracksuit top. Beside him, England's reserve goalie Ray Clemence eagerly began to help out.

65

Down came Keegan's tracksuit trousers ... but that wasn't all.

Down came the England shorts Keegan had on underneath, and...

Down came the underpants he had on under the shorts!

I KNOW THEY CALL THEIR KIT A FOOTBALL STRIP, BUT THIS IS RIDICULOUS!

Then, with Keegan thinking there wasn't anything else left to lower...

Down went his spirits. Ramsey hadn't even been calling for him! He'd been calling for another striker, Kevin Hector, to get ready.

Who knows what would have happened if Keegan had gone on? Perhaps he would have been waiting for the cross that came over and landed on Hector's head. Perhaps he would have scored with it – because Hector didn't. He put his header wide of the goal, the match ended 1–1, and England had failed to qualify for the 1974 World Cup.

Alf Ramsey lasted just two more games as manager. After a goalless draw against Portugal he was given the sack.

England's record under Alf Ramsey

Played	Won	Drawn	Lost	Goals For	Goals Ag
113	69	27	17	224	98

EARLY-BATH BOYS

Alan Mullery's sending off in 1968 may have been the first, but it certainly wasn't the last. Since then a further eight England players have been sent for an early bath. But which countries make the English see red? Here are the facts:

Argentina	2	Trevor Cherry, 1977 (tackle from behind)
		David Beckham, 1998 (deliberate powder-puff kick)
Poland	2	Alan Ball, 1973 (deliberate knee in opponent's dangly bits)
		David Batty, 1999 (late tackle)
Sweden	2	Paul Ince, 1998 (two separate fouls)
		Paul Scholes, 1999 (two separate fouls)
Austria	1	David Beckham, 2005 (two separate fouls – in 3 minutes!)
Macedonia	1	Alan Smith, 2002 (two separate fouls)
Morocco	1	Ray Wilkins, 1986 (throwing ball at referee)
Yugoslavia	1	Alan Mullery, 1968 (deliberate kick)

THE HOTSHOTS QUIZ

Geoff Hurst's goal-scoring feat with his goal-scoring feet is still a record; no other player has yet scored a hat-trick in a World Cup Final.

Here are five fantastic facts about some other England hotshots – but are they true or false?

1 Out of the nearly 1,150 footballers who've played for England, 26 of them scored a goal on their one and only appearance.

2 Out of the nearly 1,150 footballers who've played for England, five of them scored a hat-trick on their one and only appearance.

3 Bill Nicholson of Tottenham played only once for England, in a 5–2 win over Portugal in 1951 – and scored with his first touch of the game.

4 When England's Tommy Lawton scored four goals in an 8–2 win against Holland in 1946, the President of the Dutch FA told him, "Mr Lawton, you are your country's greatest centre-forward."

5 Jackie Milburn scored on his debut in 1948 (the first of the ten goals he scored in the thirteen internationals he played). He was so quick off the mark his nickname was JET.

The Top Top-Scorer Test

Here are England's top seven goalscorers and their total goals.

①	BOBBY CHARLTON	49	GOALS
②	GARY LINEKER	48	GOALS
③	JIMMY GREAVES	44	GOALS
④	MICHAEL OWEN	33	GOALS
⑤	TOM FINNEY	30	GOALS
⑥	NAT LOFTHOUSE	30	GOALS
⑦	ALAN SHEARER	30	GOALS

But if their records were worked out on average goals per game the order would change.

① NAT LOFTHOUSE
(30 GOALS IN 33 GAMES) = 0.91 GOALS PER GAME
② JIMMY GREAVES
(44 GOALS IN 57 GAMES) = 0.77 GOALS PER GAME
③ GARY LINEKER
(48 GOALS IN 80 GAMES) = 0.60 GOALS PER GAME
④ ALAN SHEARER
(30 GOALS IN 63 GAMES) = 0.48 GOALS PER GAME
⑤ BOBBY CHARLTON
(49 GOALS IN 105 GAMES) = 0.47 GOALS PER GAME
⑥ MICHAEL OWEN
(33 GOALS IN 74 GAMES) = 0.45 GOALS PER GAME
⑦ TOM FINNEY
(30 GOALS IN 76 GAMES) = 0.39 GOALS PER GAME

Of these, only Michael Owen is still playing, of course. But if he's going to make it to the top of the goals per game chart, he's got to bang 'em in even quicker than he has already. Assuming he reaches 100 games for England, he's going to have to score another 60 goals to get in front of nifty Nat Lofthouse!

And if we include another hotshot further down the list, mercurial Michael has got an even bigger challenge ahead. In eighth position in England's all-time top scorers' list is Vivian Woodward of Tottenham Hotspur and Chelsea, who scored 29 goals in his 23 internationals between 1903 and 1911. That's a rate of 1.26 goals per game. To beat him, Owen would need to score an England hat-trick every time he plays!

JOE'S JESTERS (1974)

Joe Mercer took over as England manager for just two months while the FA looked for somebody to succeed Alf Ramsey. In his playing days, jolly Joe had starred for Everton and Arsenal. He was known for having a smile that was wider than his skinny legs. Nothing could stop that smile – not even when one of his skinny legs was broken in what proved to be the last game of his career. As he was carried from the pitch on a stretcher, Joe still managed a smile and a wave for the Arsenal fans.

So it was no surprise when genial Joe called together his England players and told them:

> *Represent your country with pride. Give me pride, give me a smile. Let's have some fun.*

THE NO-SMILE, NO-PLAY AWARD...

Mike Pejic (1974, 4 caps), who, after three matches under Joe Mercer, found himself out of the England side. Why? "He never smiled," said Mercer. "I couldn't have that. It might have made the others miserable." Poor Pejic did have a bit of an excuse for not smiling, though. In his third game, against Scotland, he'd scored an own goal!

Even England's captain at that time, Emlyn Hughes (1969–1980, 62 caps), was given a telling-off. When England drew 2–2 at Wembley against tough-tackling Argentina, Hughes got into some argy-bargy with a barging Argie. Mercer criticized him afterwards, saying a captain should lead by example:

> *I want a smile on the face of English football, not a snarl.*

Down on the ground

Sometimes the fun got out of hand, though. Mercer's last match in charge was away in Yugoslavia. Arriving at the airport, some of the players started messing about on the baggage carousel. A group of security guards moved in to sort things out – and very soon after the squad discovered that they were a (short) player short. Pint-sized striker Kevin Keegan had been dragged off to be "questioned"! The security guards only released him when they found out he was an England player, but not before their "questioning" had given Keegan a few bruises. In other words, it was quite clear when he got back that the striker had been struck!

THAT'S STOPPED HIM, ALL RIGHT!

ENGLAND

Keegan struck back, though. When the match was played, he darted in to score a late goal and give England a 2–2 draw.

It was mirthful Mercer's last game in charge. The FA had found a new man to take over – and he was anything but jolly...

England's record under Joe Mercer

Played	Won	Drawn	Lost	Goals For	Goals Ag
7	3	3	1	9	7

DON'S DUDS (1974–1977)

Don Revie had been a star forward with Manchester City. How much of a star? A big enough star for them to build their whole way of playing round him. Called "The Revie Plan", it had Don drifting and dribbling just behind the forwards. It worked brilliantly, too – well enough for Manchester City to win the FA Cup in 1956.

When he finished playing, Revie came up with lots more plans – this time as manager of Leeds United. His planning guided them to titles in League, FA Cup and European competitions.

So when he became England manager, Don carried on doing what he did best: planning. The first thing he did was to draw up a plan, which included inviting a shortlist of possible England players to a meeting. The shortlist had 82 names on it!

IF THIS IS A SHORT LIST, I'D HATE TO SEE A LONG ONE!

Question: John Robertson of Nottingham Forest was one of the players on this list, but he replied to say that he wouldn't be coming to the meeting. What was his excuse?

a) He wasn't fit.

b) He wasn't a footballer.

c) He wasn't English.

THE ORGANIZING PUNCH-UPS AWARD...

Don Revie. As manager of Leeds he used to hold England v. Scotland games between his players – until he found that the rivalry was causing too many fights.

Don's dossiers

Dossiers became a very important part of pre-match preparation at this time. Scouts would go and watch the team England were due to play. They'd make a note of what the opposition players were good at, what they were bad at, what foot they preferred to kick the ball with, whether they didn't like heading the ball because it messed their hair up – everything and anything. All this information would then be put in giant dossiers and the players sent off to bed the night before a game with strict instructions to read it all before they went to sleep.

Unfortunately, not all the England players took the dossiers as seriously as they were supposed to. On one occasion, it was discovered that sheets from one of Don's dossiers had been turned over and used as scrap paper to keep score during a card game! Yes, instead of reading them, England's ace players had been playing for aces!

England all-stars: Mick Channon

Mick Channon (1972–1977, 46 caps) might just have been one of the card players. He certainly didn't think the dossiers were a great idea, saying: "players aren't really that intelligent, they don't need all that – they just want to play football."

Another scheme did appeal to him, though. Revie was keen on organizing games of bingo and carpet putting. The idea was to relax the players, but quite a few of them thought it was like being in playschool. Channon didn't. He always organized the betting – and made lots of money!

Channon was a good striker. In his England career he scored 21 goals – every one celebrated with his right arm whirling round like a windmill. There was another sport dear to his heart, though. Once, when his Southampton manager Lawrie McMenemy was giving a team talk fifteen minutes before kick-off, he realized Mick wasn't around. They found him next door, watching the horse-racing on television!

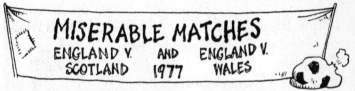

THE MAKE-A-SUCCESS-OF-YOUR-HOBBY AWARD...

Mick Channon. After he stopped galloping round football pitches, Channon became a very successful racehorse trainer. Now the horses do the galloping – but he's still organizing the betting!

MISERABLE MATCHES
ENGLAND V. SCOTLAND   AND   1977   ENGLAND V. WALES

After a bright start, England had begun to play poorly. They'd failed to get anywhere in the 1976 European Championships. In 1977, all they had to look forward to was another triumph in the British Championship...

• They beat Northern Ireland away, 2–1. No problem.
• Next it was Wales, at Wembley. Wales hadn't beaten England for 42 years. What's more, they'd *never* beaten them at Wembley. Easy, right? Wrong! Both records went as, on 31 May 1977, Wales beat England 1–0.

• Less than a week later, Scotland came to Wembley. England hadn't lost two matches in a row at Wembley – not ever. Well, they hadn't until Scotland destroyed that record by winning 2–1. To make matters even worse, at the end of the match Scots fans invaded the pitch and stole big lumps of it.

Devious Don

With England struggling to qualify for the 1978 World Cup, wretched Revie was pretty sure that the FA would soon be looking for a new manager. So what did he do?

a) Ask the FA to pay him a bonus if he left straight away.

b) Go off and find another job.

England's record under Don Revie

Played	Won	Drawn	Lost	Goals For	Goals Ag
29	14	8	7	49	25

ENGLAND FACT FILE

CLUB AND COUNTRY

In regularly changing his team, Don Revie was only following in the tradition set by the FA selection committees of course! But which clubs have supplied most international players over the years? Here are the facts about England's top eight!

CLUB	PLAYERS	APPEARANCES	ENGLAND GOALS
1 Aston Villa	64	325	78
2 Tottenham H.	58	650	171
3 Everton	57	387	86
4 Arsenal	56	723	67
5 Liverpool	55	813	113
6 Manchester Utd	54	934	165
7 Blackburn Rvrs	46	316	39
8 Chelsea	40	303	88

THE SHOCKING SHIRTS QUIZ

One of the things that Don Revie did was to introduce a controversial new England shirt. It was white with red and blue stripes on the sleeves – and for the first time ever, it carried the logo of the company that made them, Admiral.

Here are another eleven England kit firsts. Match them against the years in which they were introduced. To help, here are the years that matter:

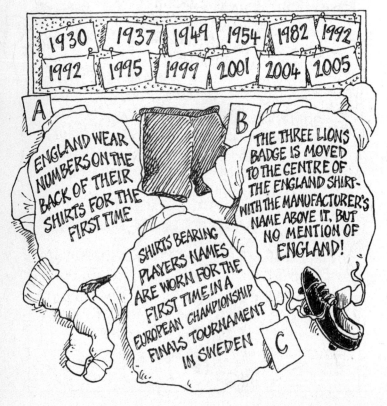

1930 1937 1949 1954 1982 1992
1992 1995 1999 2001 2004 2005

A ENGLAND WEAR NUMBERS ON THE BACK OF THEIR SHIRTS FOR THE FIRST TIME

B THE THREE LIONS BADGE IS MOVED TO THE CENTRE OF THE ENGLAND SHIRT - WITH THE MANUFACTURER'S NAME ABOVE IT, BUT NO MENTION OF ENGLAND!

C SHIRTS BEARING PLAYERS NAMES ARE WORN FOR THE FIRST TIME IN A EUROPEAN CHAMPIONSHIP FINALS TOURNAMENT IN SWEDEN

D ENGLAND SHIRTS CARRY A SINGLE GOLD STAR, TO DENOTE ENGLAND'S WORLD CUP WIN IN 1966, ABOVE THE THREE LIONS BADGE

E ENGLAND COPY THE TEAM THAT THUMPED THEM AND ADOPT LIGHTWEIGHT, V-NECK SHIRTS FOR THE FIRST TIME

F ENGLAND WEAR LIGHT BLUE SHIRTS WITH THREE BIG LIONS IN DARKER BLUE ACROSS THEIR CHESTS AND THE SHORTS ARE THE SAME STYLE

H THE MANUFACTURER'S NAME IS NO LONGER ON THE SHIRT, JUST THEIR LOGO

G AFTER PLAYING INTERNATIONALS FOR ALMOST 60 YEARS, ENGLAND INTRODUCE THEIR FIRST OFFICIAL "AWAY" SHIRTS

I ENGLAND'S SHIRTS CARRY PLAYER'S NAMES AS WELL AS NUMBERS FOR THE FIRST TIME IN A WORLD CUP QUALIFICATION MATCH

J FOR THE FIRST TIME, ENGLAND'S SHIRTS CARRY A SLOGAN

K THE THREE LIONS APPEAR ON ON THEIR OWN

L SQUAD NUMBERS APPEAR ON ENGLAND'S SHORTS FOR THE FIRST TIME

Answers:

1930 – G The shirts were either red or blue with a white collar.

1937 – A Knowing their numbers didn't help. The match was away to Scotland, and England lost 3–1.

1949 – K Before this, the three lions badge had been topped with a crown.

1954 – E When beating England 6–3 at Wembley in 1953, the great Hungarian team had worn lightweight shirts. England now did the same, throwing away their heavy flannel shirts for ever.

1982 – L Their debut was on 16 June, for England's match against France. The shorts makers were still trying to get this new-fangled innovation sorted out. Striker Paul Mariner's number had fallen off by the end of the game!

1992 – C Unfortunately, the match was a miserable 0–0 draw against Denmark, after which most of the players would have preferred not to be identified!

1992 – F Not surprisingly, they only make two appearances: for out-of-sight friendlies in Czechoslovakia and Spain.

1995 – B The shirt is made by the manufacturer Umbro. After protests, the name "England" is added beneath the badge – in smaller lettering!

THE MOST SUCCESSFUL SHIRT AWARD...
The white "home" shirt of 1995.
Wearing this, England were undefeated in sixteen games, winning eight and drawing eight.

1999 – H: To make up for it, Umbro put their name in big letters on the socks!

2001 – I: It was England's World Cup qualification 2–2 draw against Greece, on 6 October 2001. Until then names and numbers had only appeared on England shirts during World Cup and European Championship finals.

2004 – D: They were copying Brazil, Italy and Germany – each of whom have rather more stars on their shirts than England!

2005 – J: It read, "No to Racism" in white lettering on the red "away" shirt.

THE OH-NO-YOU-DON'T AWARD...

George Cohen. When the England full-back went to swap shirts after the brutal 1966 World Cup quarter-final with Argentina, angry manager Alf Ramsey refused to allow it. In the tugging match that followed, the arm of Cohen's shirt was nearly pulled off!

RON'S RUNABOUTS (1977–1982)

Ron Greenwood had been the successful manager of London side West Ham, guiding them to the FA Cup in 1964 and the European Cup Winner's Cup just a year later (the FA Cup winners qualified for the following season's Cup Winners' Cup.) Both victories were at England's home, Wembley.

THE WRITING'S-ON-THE-WALL AWARD...

Ron Greenwood had performed stylishly at Wembley long before his West Ham players made it. As a teenager, Greenwood had worked at the stadium as an apprentice signwriter!

I'LL BE BACK ONE DAY!

As a manager, Greenwood had always been ready to experiment with new ideas. Thinking about the problem of getting instructions to his team during a match, he had a radio wire laid all round the training pitch and kitted out his West Ham players with little earpieces. The practice match began nicely. Radio Ron stayed on air for a complete half, with

Greenwood happily talking to his players as they ran around. Then, during the half-time break, everything suddenly went dead. Taking the chance to do a bit of grass-cutting, the groundsman had sliced through the radio wire with his lawnmower!

England all-Stars: Viv Anderson

Question: One of Ron Greenwood's selections, Viv Anderson, was the 936th footballer to be picked for England. What was it about him that was different to the previous 935?

ⓐ HIS LEGS   ⓑ HIS SKIN   ⓒ HIS HEART

Answer: b) When he ran out at Wembley on the evening of 29 November 1978 as right-back for the 1–0 win over Czechoslovakia, Viv (short for Vivian) Anderson became the first black player to be selected for England.

Anderson's legs were pretty special, too. They were so long and good at tackling he was nicknamed "the spider".

ANDERSON'S GOT HIS WINGER TRAPPED BY THE CORNER FLAG...

It had taken a long time to happen. Anderson was a terrific full-back, but being a terrific footballer hadn't helped in the past. A black striker named Jack Leslie, who banged in over 130 goals in 400 appearances for Plymouth in the 1920s and 30s had once been selected for England – only to be told a mistake had been made. The selectors had been fooled by the fact that he'd been born in London and hadn't realized Leslie wasn't white.

Although versatile Viv Anderson's club career sparkled – he won loads of trophies with Nottingham Forest, Arsenal and Manchester United – his time with England had its share of disappointments. Between 1978 and 1988 he won 30 caps. In 1982 and 1986, though, he set a record he would rather not have: going to two successive World Cups and not getting on the pitch once.

Even so, he became a role-model for thousands of other youngsters. Since that night at Wembley, over 50 black players have represented England – and it was All-Star Anderson who'd led the way.

Tournament tears, part 1

England failed to reach the World Cup finals in 1978. They did better for the European Championships two years later and, in 1980, headed for the finals in Italy. England's group games ended in a win, a draw and a defeat – not good enough to get them any further in the competition. Of the three games, though, it was the drawn match that produced the most tears...

Crowd trouble during England's opening match against Belgium led to the Italian police firing tear gas. Unfortunately, they hadn't checked to see which way the wind was blowing. Clouds of the stuff drifted on to the pitch and England's goalkeeper, Ray Clemence, suddenly found himself unable to see the ball for crying.

But even more tears were on the way...

England's progress in qualifying for the 1982 World Cup finals hadn't been too good. They travelled to play part-timers Norway desperate for a win ... and lost. After leading 1–0, Norway were allowed to come back and win 2–1.

Bjørge Lillelien, a Norwegian TV commentator. At the end of the match he raved:

Lord Nelson, Lord Beaverbrook, Sir Winston Churchill, Sir Anthony Eden, Clement Atlee, Henry Cooper, Lady Diana. We have beaten them all, we have beaten them all! Maggie Thatcher, can you hear me? Your boys took a hell of a beating! Your boys took a hell of a beating!

In 2002 this was voted by *The Observer* newspaper the Greatest Bit of Commentary Ever!

Back in England, the newspapers were raving too: raving mad! "England are virtually out of the World Cup," said *The Sun* newspaper. "Now we say that's the only course for Ron – out".

Tournament tears, part 2

Gloomy Greenwood wasn't very happy himself. On the aeroplane home he decided that he was going to resign. Who talked him out of it?

a) The players.
b) The newspaper reporters.
c) Mrs Greenwood.

Soon every England fan was crying – with delight! To stand a chance of qualifying for the 1982 World Cup finals, England needed to beat Hungary in their final match and hope Switzerland came to their aid by beating Romania ... and they did just that! Grateful Greenwood showed just how grateful he was by fishing out a tie he'd bought in Switzerland and wearing it for a week!

RON, SURELY YOU CAN TAKE IT OFF AT NIGHT?

MAGIC MATCHES
ENGLAND V FRANCE
1982

England had a dream start to the 1982 World Cup tournament. Here's how you could recreate the moment in a game with your mates:
• Straight from the kick-off, hit the ball down the right wing and win a throw about ten metres from France's goal line.

• Have somebody pretend to be Steve Coppell, England's right-winger. He snatches the ball up and takes a quick throw to...

• The person pretending to be England defender, Terry Butcher, who heads it on to...

• Whoever's lucky enough to be playing the part of England midfield dynamo Bryan Robson. He races into the penalty area and lashes the ball into the net!

• Check your watches. If all that's taken longer than the 27 seconds England needed then you have to go back and do it again.

• The person playing Bryan Robson gets doubly lucky. After the game you have to do what the World Cup organizers did ... and present him with a gold watch!

• France have to come back to equalize after 24 minutes, but another goal from Robson in the second half and one from striker Paul Mariner seven minutes from the end give England a 3–1 win.

WARNING: DO NOT DO THIS BIT!
Afterwards, England midfielder Graham Rix sought out the famous French captain Michel Platini in search of a souvenir of the match ... and the two players swapped shorts!

The reign in Spain...

Unfortunately, the rest of England's tournament wasn't as successful. They won through to the next stage which, unlike nowadays, wasn't a knockout stage but a second round of league matches. They drew 0–0 with West Germany then, when they had to win by a two-goal margin, they could manage only another goalless draw against host country Spain. England were out, after five games – and no defeats!

Greenwood promptly resigned.

England's record under Ron Greenwood

Played	Won	Drawn	Lost	Goals For	Goals Ag
55	33	12	10	93	40

SNAPPY STRIKERS

Bryan Robson's snappy strike in the 1982 World Cup was a quick goal. It was something he made so much of a habit during his career that he should have been called rapid-fire Robson! But was his 1982 goal the quickest? Have other England goals been even more snappily scored? Here are the facts!

1 Tommy Lawton (Chelsea) 17 secs v. Portugal, 1947 won 10-0

2 Bryan Robson (Man. Utd) 27 secs v. France, 1982 won 3-1

3 John Cock (Huddersfield)30 secs v. Ireland, 1919 drew 1-1

4 Bill Nicholson (Tottenham H.)30 secs v. Portugal, 1951 won 5-2

5 Tommy Lawton (Chelsea) 34 secs v. Belgium, 1947 won 5-2

6 Edgar Chadwick (Everton)35 secs v. Scotland, 1892 won 4-1

7 Gareth Southgate (Middlesbrough) 36 secs v. South Africa, 2003 won 2-1

8 Bryan Robson (Man. Utd) 38 secs v. Yugoslavia, 1989 won 2-1

9 Gary Lineker (Tottenham H.) 42 secs v. Malaysia, 1991 won 4-2

10 Bryan Robson (Man. Utd) 44 secs v. N. Ireland, 1982 won 4-0

BOBBY'S BATTLERS (1982–1990)

Bobby Robson was the next man
to sit in the England manager's chair. He'd had plenty
of experience. He'd played 20 times for England
himself then, like awesome Alf Ramsey before him,
gone on to win trophies as manager of Ipswich Town.

Robson was a great talker – but sometimes Bobby's
babbling got him into trouble...

- When football hooligans caused trouble during an
  Ipswich match at Millwall, he said his solution
  would be to turn flame-throwers on them!

- His team talks could go on for ages. He once called
  the England players together ten minutes before
  dinner time – and was still talking three hours later.

- Robson was also famous for forgetting his player's
  names. He once greeted his captain, Bryan Robson,
  at breakfast with, "Good morning, Bobby!"

TEAM SHEET

- MICKEY MOUSE
- NODDY
- PRINCE CHARLES
- THE SHORT GUY WITH THE HAIRY EARS
- SCOOBY-DOO

LOOKS LIKE BOBBY'S HAVING ONE OF HIS BAD DAYS!

Bad beginnings

England didn't start very well under Bobby Robson. They lost six of their first 20 games, which was a worse record than any previous England manager. One bright spot, though, was a European Championship qualifier against little Luxembourg in 1984. England won 9–0, which produced a classic bit of Bobby-babble: "Well, we got nine and you can't score more than that".

THE BOOT'S-ON-THE-OTHER-FOOT AWARD...

Tony Woodcock (1978–1986, 42 caps). In 1982, the Nottingham Forest and Arsenal striker had helped give Robson his first win, hitting a first-minute goal in a 3–0 win against Greece ... while wearing borrowed boots.

A bad defeat at Wembley against Denmark led to England failing to reach the 1984 European Championship finals. As the team set off for a summer tour to South America, it all looked bleak. Then...

MAGIC MATCHES
BRAZIL V ENGLAND
1984

Brazil hadn't been beaten at home for 25 years. England hadn't beaten them, home or away, for 28 years. So what happened? England won, 2–0!

The highlight of the game was England's first goal, scored by John Barnes (1983–1996, 79 caps). Try it in your next school match. Here's how:

• Get the ball on the left wing, about 35 metres from goal.

• Cut inside your full-back.

• Cut inside another defender.

• And another.

• And another. You're in the penalty area now.

• Another defender (ideally, one as good as Brazil's Junior) comes in to tackle you. Pretend to shoot – but don't! Your defender-cum-Junior goes the wrong way!

• Out races the goalkeeper (as good or better than Brazil's Roberto Costa, if possible). He's about to whip the ball off your toe…

• But before he can, you slide it under his body.

John Barnes' goal was so good it was shown for months afterwards on Brazilian TV! They reckoned it was just as good a goal as their team could score.

MISERABLE MATCHES
ARGENTINA V ENGLAND
1986

Two years later, England battled their way into the finals of the 1986 World Cup. In the quarter-finals they met Argentina – and fans all over the world were treated to a goal as good as that from John Barnes. Unfortunately for England, it was scored by Diego Maradona of Argentina, who dribbled his way past defender after defender in a run from the halfway line, before banging the ball past England's goalkeeper Peter Shilton.

That goal, which made the score 2–0, has been shown a lot on TV – but nothing like as much as Argentina's first goal, also "scored" by Maradona, four minutes earlier.

DO NOT DO THIS IN YOUR NEXT SCHOOL MATCH!

• Wait for a high-spinning miskick to head towards the other team's goal.
• Race in and leap as high as you can...
• But because the ball's higher and the goalie's going to punch it away...
• Punch it yourself – into the goal!
• Run around like a mad thing so that the referee and linesman think you couldn't possibly have done anything wrong.

96

England were out, and Maradona's same cheating hand went on to lift the World Cup.

THE BEST LOO DECORATION AWARD...

Kenny Sansom (1979–1988, 86 caps).
England's left-back against Argentina that day has a huge poster showing Maradona's handball goal. It hangs in his loo!

Robson's rubbish

The newspapers were once quite kind to England managers. If the team played badly, it was the players' fault. No longer. It was now the manager's fault for not picking the players the newspapers wanted to see in the team. Here are some of the comments aimed at Bobby Robson:

⚽ *Robson's Rubbish*, said *The Sun* after England had been beaten by Denmark in 1983.

⚽ *Robson Out, Clough In*, proclaimed *The Sun*'s specially produced badges after Wales had beaten England 1–0 in 1984. Derby's manager Brian Clough was the man the newspaper was supporting. There was nothing shady going on, of course. The fact that Clough's biography was later written by a *Sun* reporter was pure coincidence!

⚽ *Robson Must Go!* cried the *Daily Mirror* after Scotland's 1–0 victory over England in 1985 ... ignoring the fact that the defeat was the team's first in nine matches!

⚽ *Despair!* shouted just about every newspaper after England had lost one and drawn in their first two matches in the 1986 World Cup finals. Robson was pictured leaning miserably on the balcony of his hotel room with his hands over his ears. What the papers didn't say was that the manager was listening to his personal stereo!

⚽ *Robson Lionhearts Are On The March!* the same papers hypocritically crowed just 24 hours later, after England had walloped Poland to qualify from their 1986 World Cup group!

⚽ *On Yer Bike, Robson!* shouted *The Sun* after England had lost 1–0 to the Irish Republic in Euro '88.

⚽ *England Mustafa New Boss*, cried the same newspaper when the team drew 1–1 with Saudi Arabia in November 1988. Less than two years later, almost the same players reached the semi-finals of the 1990 World Cup!

England all-stars: Gary Lineker

Gary Lineker (1984–1992, 80 caps) was one of England's best-ever strikers. He'd won the "golden boot" top-scorer's trophy at the 1986 World Cup and was hoping to do it again in 1990. He'd also been England's penalty-taker for the past four years.

Question: How many penalties had Lineker taken for England up until 1990

ⓐ FEWER THAN 3   ⓑ 3 TO 5   ⓒ MORE THAN 5

Answer: a) As fewer than three as it was possible to get. Not two, or one – but none! He hadn't spotted a spot-kick once.

And then, in England's quarter-final match against Cameroon, two came along together. Number one came just six minutes from the end of full time, with England losing 1–2! As Gary placed the ball on the penalty spot, into his mind flashed two thoughts. The first thought was of his nervous brother – and how he'd be watching the game with his hands over his eyes!

99

The second thought was more useful. Lineker used to take twenty practice penalties every day, putting them in the same spot every time. Remembering this, goal-den Gary told himself to do exactly the same. He did – and scored, to make it 2–2 and take the game into extra time.

That was when the second penalty came along, after Lineker was fouled. He banged that one in, too, to give England a 3–2 win.

Sadly, lethal Lineker's penalty practice didn't help him two years later, in a friendly match against Russia in April, 1992. Needing just one more goal to become equal all-time England top scorer (with Bobby Charlton), along came another penalty. Up stepped gleeful Gary ... only to become glum Gary as he missed. His England career ended a few games later without him scoring that one elusive goal.

 ☆ *MAGIC-MISERABLE* MATCH
ENGLAND V WEST GERMANY 1990

Thanks to Gary Lineker's two penalties against Cameroon, England made it through to the semi-finals of the 1990 World Cup. There they met West Germany in a game that was by turns magic and miserable:

Miserable: Germany go ahead with a lucky goal. From a free kick the ball takes a deflection, flies high into the air ... then down into the England net!

Magic: Ten minutes from the end, Lineker scores to put England level.

Miserable: In extra time, England's Chris Waddle hits the post.

Magic: Germany's Guido Buchwald hits the post as well!

Miserable: Paul Gascoigne of England gets a yellow card. It means he'll miss the final if England get there. He's in tears.

Totally, completely and utterly miserable: England lose 4–3 in a penalty shoot-out.

I'M MISERABLE BECAUSE WE LOST, BUT I'D HAVE BEEN JUST AS MISERABLE IF WE'D WON!

England all-stars: Paul Gascoigne

Gascoigne (1988–1998, 57 caps) was a beefy midfielder with a lot of skill. England manager Bobby Robson also once said that Gascoigne was – what?
a) As thick as a plank.
b) As daft as a brush.
c) As mad as a hatter.

Answer: b) – to which Gascoigne responded by turning up for training next day with a hairbrush tucked down the side of his sock!

He was also very generous. Alan Shearer tells the story of how Gascoigne saw a youngster hanging around the team hotel. What did Gazza give him?

(a) HIS SHIRT (b) HIS SHORTS (c) HIS SOCKS

Answer: a), b) and c) – and his boots as well! Gascoigne was a practical joker. In the run-up to the 1990 World Cup, Robson's team had a spate of injuries. The manager was worried – and never more so than when a pathetic Paul staggered towards him in the team hotel covered in bandages and dripping blood. Except that the bandages were hotel serviettes and the blood was tomato sauce!

THE TALENT-SPOTTING (NOT!) AWARD...

Bobby Robson – who, during his time as manager of Ipswich Town, rejected a chunky fifteen-year-old triallist named ... Paul Gascoigne.

Bobby's bye-bye

Robson's record as England manager was pretty good. Under him, England qualified for two World Cups, reaching the quarter-final in one and the semi-final in the other, both times being knocked out by the winners.

He also offered to resign twice – once after the 1986 World Cup, and again after England had performed poorly in the 1988 European Championships. Both times the FA had turned him down.

So it baffled Bobby that, just before the team went off for the 1990 World Cup, the FA said they'd be looking for a new manager to take charge when the tournament was over. After eight years, Robson had to find himself another job – which he did, with the Dutch league club PSV Eindhoven.

Question: What did newspapers say this time?

Answer: c) After spending eight years telling Robson to retire, when he did they didn't like it!

In 2002, Sir Bobby Robson received a knighthood for his services to football. The newspaper reporters are still waiting for theirs.

England's record under Bobby Robson

Played	Won	Drawn	Lost	Goals For	Goals Ag
95	47	30	18	154	60

ENGLAND FACT FILE

FAVOURITE FOES

Nowadays, with all the European Championship and World Cup matches, the teams England come up against are determined by the luck of the draw. If they could choose, though, who would England like to face? Their favourite foes, of course – the teams they always beat. And who are they? Here are the favourite facts!

England have always beaten these countries:
Albania (4 times), Azerbaijan (2), Bohemia (1), Canada (1), China (1), Cyprus (2), Ecuador (1), Egypt (2), Georgia (2), Kuwait (1), Liechtenstein (2), Luxembourg (9), Malaysia (1), Malta (3), Moldova (2), New Zealand (2), Paraguay (2), San Marino (2), Serbia and Montenegro (1), Slovakia (2), South Africa (2), Ukraine (2).

THE PERILOUS PENALTIES QUIZ

The penalty shoot-out that Bobby Robson's England lost at the 1990 World Cup marked the beginning of a shocking shoot-out sequence:

World Cup '90 semi-final
v. Germany: Drew 1-1,
LOST 3-4 on penalties

Euro '96 quarter-final v. Spain:
Drew 0-0, WON 4-2 on penalties

Euro '96 semi-final v. Germany:
Drew 1-1, LOST 5-6 on penalties

World Cup '98 round 2
v. Argentina: Drew 2-2
LOST 3-4 on penalties

Euro 2004 quarter-final
v. Portugal: Drew 2-2
LOST 5-6 on penalties!

So, how do you feel about trying a penalties quiz? As nervous as an England penalty-taker? Don't worry. Just take a deep breath ... then match the twitching ten England penalty-takers over the page with the details about them.

GEOFF HURST
The 1966 hat-trick hero had a powerful penalty-taking technique

ALLAN CLARKE
A brave first-time penalty taker

FRANCIS LEE
He scored so many penalties for his club, Manchester City, that he was nicknamed 'Lee won pen'. Not for England sadly

GARY LINEKER
He believed that practice made perfect

STUART PEARCE
Didn't get all steamed up about penalties

GARETH SOUTHGATE
He hoped he'd be luckier than he was first time

DAVID BATTY
Must have been mad to think he could score in the World Cup 1998 shoot-out

ALAN SHEARER
Ever-dependable Geordie kicker

MICHAEL OWEN
A striker who's always eager to learn

DAVID BECKHAM
Captain who's always happy to be put on the spot

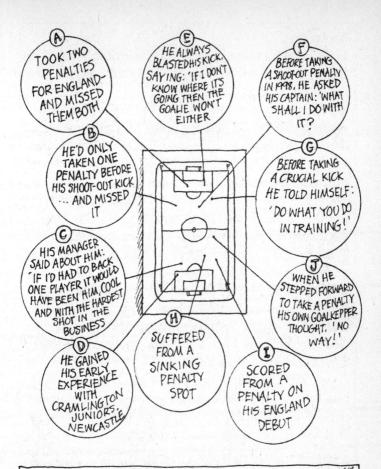

A. TOOK TWO PENALTIES FOR ENGLAND – AND MISSED THEM BOTH

B. HE'D ONLY TAKEN ONE PENALTY BEFORE HIS SHOOT-OUT KICK ... AND MISSED IT

C. HIS MANAGER SAID ABOUT HIM: 'IF I'D HAD TO BACK ONE PLAYER IT WOULD HAVE BEEN HIM, COOL AND WITH THE HARDEST SHOT IN THE BUSINESS

D. HE GAINED HIS EARLY EXPERIENCE WITH CRAMLINGTON JUNIORS, NEWCASTLE

E. HE ALWAYS BLASTED HIS KICK, SAYING: 'IF I DON'T KNOW WHERE IT'S GOING THEN THE GOALIE WON'T EITHER

F. BEFORE TAKING A SHOOT-OUT PENALTY IN 1998, HE ASKED HIS CAPTAIN: 'WHAT SHALL I DO WITH IT?'

G. BEFORE TAKING A CRUCIAL KICK HE TOLD HIMSELF: 'DO WHAT YOU DO IN TRAINING!'

H. SUFFERED FROM A SINKING PENALTY SPOT

I. SCORED FROM A PENALTY ON HIS ENGLAND DEBUT

J. WHEN HE STEPPED FORWARD TO TAKE A PENALTY HIS OWN GOALKEEPER THOUGHT, 'NO WAY!'

🏆 THE POP-STAR'S PENALTY-WATCHING AWARD...

The Rolling Stones – who, during a concert taking place at the same time as the 1990 World Cup penalty shoot-out against Germany, left the stage to watch the kicks, then came back and continued where they left off.

Answers:

1–E: Hurst's technique usually worked. In a 5–0 friendly against France in 1969 he scored two penalties in another hat-trick.

2–I: Not only did Allan Clarke (1970–75, 19 caps) volunteer to take a penalty in his first international, it gave England a 1–0 win in a 1970 World Cup finals group match against Czechoslovakia.

3–A: Lee's second miss, against Portugal at Wembley, was a disaster: he stumbled as he ran up to take the kick and hit it wide!

4–G: And he did, scoring two vital penalties in the 1990 World Cup quarter-final against Cameroon and netting his kick in the shoot-out.

5–C: So said Bobby Robson after sick Stuart was first to miss in the 1990 shoot-out. Plucky Pearce later proved his manager right, though, scoring with his kicks in both the Euro '96 shoot-outs.

6–B: Southgate missed the vital kick in the Euro '96 shoot-out. His only other penalty, in a league game, had hit the post. Talking before the game about the prospect of taking another penalty he'd said: "I think I'd be more comfortable than I was then"!

THE YOU'VE-GOT-TO-LAUGH-ABOUT-IT AWARD...

Tony Adams, England's captain at Euro 96. With nobody knowing what to say that would make Southgate feel better, he put an arm round him and said bluntly, "But Gareth, it was a rubbish penalty, wasn't it?" Southgate had to laugh.

7–J: The goalkeeper, David Seaman, was spot-on (ho-ho). Batty had never scored a penalty in a senior game, not one – for the simple reason he'd never taken a penalty in a senior game! His kick was saved.

8–D: He scored every shoot-out penalty he took.

9–F: And Alan Shearer replied, "stick it in the net like you usually do." So he did.

10–H: As he went to strike the ball during the Euro 2004 shoot-out against Portugal, the soft ground around the penalty spot caused him to miscue. Instead of the ball going up then dipping sharply down as it does with his free kicks, this one went up … and up … high into the stand behind the goal!

THE ALTERNATIVES - TO - THE PENALTY - SHOOT - OUT AWARD...

The disappearing team. As an alternative to penalty shoot-outs to decide games that are level at the end of full-time, it's been suggested that teams should play extra time until one of them scores – and to make goals more likely, players from each side should go off every few minutes until only the goalies are left!

TAYLOR'S TURNIPS (1990–1993)

Do you think you'd like to be England manager one day? Well, check out your school reports to see if they say something like this: "Graham shows great enthusiasm for sport and is organizing the football."

The "Graham" in question was Graham Taylor, the man who followed Bobby Robson as manager of England.

This was a really accurate report (proof that teachers do know what they're talking about!) because Taylor turned out to be a better organizer than a player. He never won an England cap, playing in the lower leagues with Grimsby Town and Lincoln City. But when he turned to management, after having to stop playing because of a badly injured hip, he was very successful with club sides Lincoln, Watford and Aston Villa.

Question: Taylor was another manager who would spout on for hours. What did one of his players call him?
a) Tommy-Gun Taylor.
b) The Fastest Tongue in the West.
c) The Galloping Gabbler.

Answer b) In other words, talkative Taylor had gone from having the slowest hip to the fastest lip!

THE FAMOUS CAROL-SINGER'S AWARD...

Graham Taylor. One December evening, when he was manager of Watford, groovy Graham went out for the evening with the club's chairman. When the pair returned, after too many drinks, they went around Taylor's neighbours carol-singing ... and did brilliantly. Why? Because Watford's chairman was pop-singer Elton John!

Taylor-made tactics

A feature of Taylor's tactics with his club sides had been the "long ball" – that is, asking his players not to mess about with short passes but bang it up into the air and towards the other team's goal as quickly as possible.

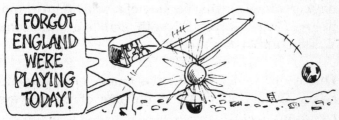

I FORGOT ENGLAND WERE PLAYING TODAY!

Here's what England goalkeeper David Seaman said the players were asked to do. Try it in your next school match and see how effective it is ... or isn't.

- It's your kick-off. The whistle blows...
- Have the person taking the kick-off tap it to the player beside them...
- Who then boots it into touch as far down the pitch as they can.

- Congratulate yourselves! You've just played like England!

The tactic was supposed to put the other team on the defensive by getting the ball into their half. Unfortunately, all they did was throw the ball to their goalkeeper to boot back into England's half!

England all-stars: Stuart Pearce

Stuart Pearce (1987–1999, 78 caps) couldn't only hammer the ball out of play, he could hammer opposing wingers too! The 999th player to be capped in England's history, he was a left back with a fearsome tackle.

Question: What was Pearce's nickname?

Answer: a) Which is short for "psychopath", meaning "a person who is liable to behave violently in getting his own way". You did not want to be tackled by Stuart Pearce!

Mind you, perilous penalties and frightful free kicks dotted Pearce's career so much that a better nickname might have been "penalized" Pearce:
- He had a late free-kick goal disallowed against Holland in the 1990 World Cup finals.

• He had his kick saved in that tournament's penalty shoot-out.
• When Taylor's team met France in the Euro '92 finals, he had a free-kick goal disallowed yet again, with another one smashing against the French crossbar.
• He was one of those who scored his penalty, four years later during Euro '96, in a shoot-out against Spain.
• In his final league game before he retired, poor Pearce stepped up to take a penalty which would give him 100 league goals in his career. He missed.

Headline horrors

England didn't do well under Graham Taylor. In fact, they did unbelievably badly. Everybody was unhappy about it – except the know-it-all newspapers, of course. They were happy that Taylor's torment was giving them the chance to come up with their most insulting headlines...

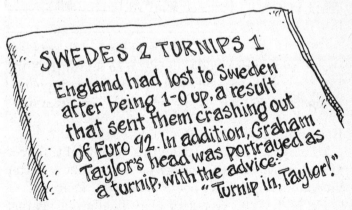

SWEDES 2 TURNIPS 1
England had lost to Sweden after being 1-0 up, a result that sent them crashing out of Euro 92. In addition, Graham Taylor's head was portrayed as a turnip, with the advice:
"Turnip in, Taylor!"

SPANISH 1 ONIONS 0
England's next game saw them lose a friendly, 1-0 away to Spain.

NORSE MANURE!
Was the stinking head-line after a terrible 2-0 defeat away to Norway, which virtually meant that England wouldn't qualify for the 1994 World Cup finals.

YANKS 2 PLANKS 0
England's next game was an even worse defeat, 2-0 against USA.

MISERABLE MATCHES
HOLLAND V ENGLAND
1993

This was the match England had to win if they were going to qualify for the 1994 World Cup finals. But lose it they did, 2–0.

For once, though, everybody agreed that the team had been treated badly. In the first half, midfielder David Platt was through with only the Dutch goalkeeper to beat, when he was dragged to the ground by their defender and captain, Ronald Koemann. Said rotten Ronald after the match:

I expected to see the red card.

But he didn't see any card at all, and the free kick England were awarded was charged down by the encroaching Dutch defenders.

Into the second half, and Holland won a free kick. They took it ... and it was charged down by encroaching England defenders. This time, though, the referee insisted that the kick be taken again!

It was – by the same Ronald Koemann who should have been taking an early bath – and he scored! Holland were on their way to victory.

TV tantrums

The miserable match against Holland was certainly miserable for the fans – but it proved to be even more miserable for manager Graham Taylor. Why?

a) He'd agreed to write about the game for the newspapers.

b) He'd agreed to talk about it on TV.

c) He'd said he'd resign if England didn't win.

Answer: b) Worse than that, even – he'd agreed to take part in a documentary programme and have a microphone attached to him in the England dug-out so that viewers could hear every word he said!

115

THE SWEAR-BOX AWARD...

Graham Taylor and Channel 4 TV (shared). Quite a few of those words were four-lettered swear words starting with "F". Grimacing Graham later moaned: "The programme was made over 18 months and during that time I must have said that word 27 times – and every single one was left in!"

Viewers were treated to a few non-swearing comments as well. Here are the words of one Taylor sentence, uttered during the 2–0 defeat by Norway, when glum Graham had seen something he disapproved of. Sort these words into the order in which he used them: DO I NOT LIKE THAT

Answer: Sorry, that was a trick question. They're in the right order already! Why tongue-tied Taylor said "Do I not like that" instead of "I don't like that" is a mystery, but the words went on to become a national catchphrase. It's now so well known that you'll find it in dictionaries of quotations.

But Taylor's biggest moan during the programme came when rotten Ronald Koemann scored with his free kick. Complaining that the Dutch captain should have been sent off for his first-half foul, he ranted at the referee's assistant, "Your friend out there has cost me my job!"

He was right. Within a week, England were looking for a new manager.

England's record under Graham Taylor

Played	Won	Drawn	Lost	Goals For	Goals Ag
38	18	13	7	62	32

ENGLAND FACT FILE

FEARED FOES

You've already had the facts about the teams England love to meet, because they always beat them — but what about those they don't like to meet, those they want to avoid at all costs because they've not won even half their games against them? Here are the fearful facts!

England's worst performances have been against these countries:
Brazil (only 3 wins in 21 games)
West Germany (11 wins in 25 games)
Italy (7 wins in 22 games)
Holland (5 wins in 16 games)
Romania (2 wins in 11 games)
Scotland (45 wins in 110 games)
Sweden (6 wins in 20 games)

Favourite AND feared foes
There are two countries that England have never beaten — but they've never lost to them either:
Saudi Arabia (2 draws in 2 games)
South Korea (1 draw in 1 game).

TERRY'S TIGERS (1994–1996)

It was becoming harder and harder to find somebody prepared to take on the job of England manager. Steve Coppell, ex-England winger and the early favourite said:

> *I don't want the job and I don't envy the one who gets it.*

Englishman Roy Hodgson, then manager of Switzerland, wasn't interested:

> *You have got to be joking!*

Terry Venables was the man who got the job. Fortunately, he wanted it – and, as a TV pundit, had shown himself to be fond of a joke. He was also an ex-player.

Question: For which of the following teams had Terry Venables won caps during his playing career?
a) England Schoolboys.
b) England Youth.
c) England Amateur.
d) England Under-23s.
e) England full international.

Answer: All of them. Venables was the first player to complete a full set of caps for England at every possible level.

Terry's tactics

Venables was the first England manager to be dubbed a "coach" rather than a "manager". He said:

We must have a system the players understand. It's up to me to make it as simple as possible.

REPEAT AFTER ME: 'G' IS FOR 'GOAL'

England had already qualified for the next big tournament – the European Championships in 1996 – as hosts. This gave Venables a chance to work on his tactics during lots of friendly games.

Question: Which of these was a Terry tactic?
a) The Christmas-cracker formation.
b) The Christmas-tree formation.
c) The Christmas-turkey formation.

> **Answer: b)** It was a line-up of goalkeeper, four defenders, three midfielders, two middle-forwards and a lone striker.

England all-star: David Seaman

David Seaman (1988–2002, 75 caps) was England's goalkeeper. His long international career had begun in an away game against Saudi Arabia – on a very dodgy pitch. The match had been delayed until the evening so that it wasn't too hot, but that was also the time of day when the local insects came out to play. Seaman found himself diving around a penalty area covered with huge bugs!

Seaman became a penalty-saving hero for England during Euro '96. In only their second match – a group game against Scotland – Seaman was faced with a penalty. In ran Scotland's Gary McAllister, only to see Seaman save his kick by pushing it over the crossbar with his left elbow!

Question: Seaman later said that what followed was enough to put him off saving any more penalties. What was he referring to?

a) The howling of the Scots fans.

b) The comments of the referee.

c) The congratulations of his captain.

> **Answer: c)** Captain and fellow Arsenal teammate Tony Adams rushed up and gave him a great big kiss!

In the quarter-finals, Seaman did it again, making two saves during a penalty shoot-out against Spain.

By the time England were beaten, in another shoot-out by Germany in the semi-final, David Seaman had become a national hero. When he went to watch the tennis at Wimbledon shortly after the tournament ended, the tennis stopped while everybody applauded him!

Seaman would have a few slip-ups in later years (such as letting a long-range free kick from Ronaldinho go over his head against Brazil in the 2002 World Cup quarter finals) but under manager Venables he was one of Terry's Tigers!

THE RETIRED -GOALKEEPER'S- SLIP-UP AWARD...

David Seaman – who, in 2004, put on a pair of skates to take part in a TV programme called *Strictly Ice Dancing*.

Holland were in England's group during Euro '96. After the agony of losing to them in their 1994 World Cup qualifier, the last thing England wanted was to lose to them again. They didn't. Before their first group game against Switzerland, the players had watched videos of Holland in action. Before their match against Scotland they'd watched videos of Holland in action. And before this game – well, you can guess. No wonder England had a pair of "fast forwards"...

23 MINUTES – ALAN SHEARER SCORES A PENALTY

51 MINUTES – TEDDY SHERINGHAM SCORES WITH A HEADER

57 MINUTES – SHEARER SCORES HIS SECOND GOAL

62 MINUTES – SHERINGHAM SCORED HIS SECOND GOAL

Question: Towards the end of the game, Holland scored a consolation goal to make the score 4–1, but even this made England fans cheer. Why?

a) It went through David Seaman's legs.

b) It made Scots fans cry.

c) It hit the referee on the bum.

them.

because Holland had scored one more goal than
that Scotland were knocked out of the tournament
Answer: b) – although it did **a)** as well. It meant

Ta-ta Terry

You would have thought, after losing Bobby Robson following England's run to the World Cup semi-finals in 1990, that England wouldn't want to lose another successful manager. Wrong. Venables, who'd been having business problems, wasn't offered another contract by the FA

England were once again without a coach/driver!

England's record under Terry Venables

Played	Won	Drawn	Lost	Goals For	Goals Ag
23	11	11	7	35	13

SUPER STOPPERS

David Seaman was hot stuff when it came to dealing with penalties – but was stopper Seaman the best? How does he compare to other England goalies when it comes to penalties given away during a match, not in a shoot-out? Has a prouder penalty-stopper worn the goalkeeping jersey for England? Who was the most pathetic penalty person to stand between the England goalposts?

Here are the facts!
Goalkeepers facing more than two penalties during their England careers

1 Harry Hibbs (1929–1936) 3 penalties 0 let in 100% success!
2 Ron Springett (1959–1966) 3 penalties 1 let in 67% success
3 David Seaman (1988–2002) 3 penalties 2 let in 33% success
3 Nigel Martyn (1992–2002) 3 penalties 2 let in 33% success
3 Sam Hardy (1907–1920) 3 penalties 2 let in 33% success
6 Gordon Banks (1963–1972) 5 penalties 4 let in 20% success
6 David James (1997–2005) 5 penalties 4 let in 20% success
8 Ray Clemence (1972–1983) 8 penalties 7 let in 12% success
9 Peter Shilton (1970–1990) 15 penalties 14 let in 7% success
10 Gil Merrick (1951–54) 3 penalties 3 let in 0% success

But how did they do apart from penalties? Here are the same goalkeepers judged on the games in which they didn't let a goal in!

1 David Seaman 40 clean sheets in 75 games 54%
2 Peter Shilton 66 clean sheets in 125 games 53%
2 Nigel Martyn 12 clean sheets in 23 games 53%

4 Gordon Banks 35 clean sheets in 73 games 48%
5 Ray Clemence 27 clean sheets in 61 games 45%
6 Harry Hibbs 10 clean sheets in 25 games 40%
7 David James 12 clean sheets in 33 games 37%
8 Sam Hardy 7 clean sheets in 21 games 34%
9 Ron Springett 7 clean sheets in 33 games 22%
10 Gil Merrick 5 clean sheets in 23 games 22%

THE SILLY SONGS QUIZ

Over the years some of England's footballers may have been foul, but never as foul as the pop songs that have accompanied them on their travels. The "singing" (especially when it's been by the players themselves) has often sounded more like the howling of a pack of wild dogs.

So ... here's a Top Ten chart of football songs. To reveal the real titles or lyrics, replace the word HOWLING by one of these: *feet, head, home, how, playing, Queen, rest, three, time, Willy*

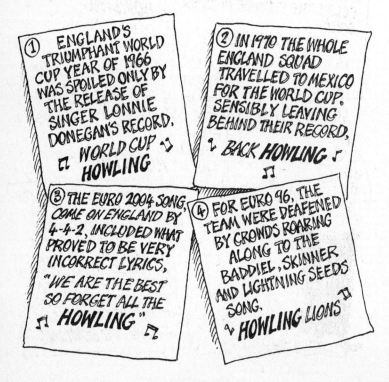

① ENGLAND'S TRIUMPHANT WORLD CUP YEAR OF 1966 WAS SPOILED ONLY BY THE RELEASE OF SINGER LONNIE DONEGAN'S RECORD, WORLD CUP HOWLING

② IN 1970 THE WHOLE ENGLAND SQUAD TRAVELLED TO MEXICO FOR THE WORLD CUP, SENSIBLY LEAVING BEHIND THEIR RECORD, BACK HOWLING

③ THE EURO 2004 SONG, COME ON ENGLAND BY 4-4-2, INCLUDED WHAT PROVED TO BE VERY INCORRECT LYRICS, "WE ARE THE BEST SO FORGET ALL THE HOWLING"

④ FOR EURO 96, THE TEAM WERE DEAFENED BY CROWDS ROARING ALONG TO THE BADDIEL, SKINNER AND LIGHTNING SEEDS SONG, HOWLING LIONS

⑤ ONE OF THE BEST FOOTBALL SONGS WAS NEW ORDER'S *WORLD IN MOTION* FOR THE 1990 WORLD CUP... AT LEAST IT WAS UNTIL IT REACHED THE PART WHERE ENGLAND WINGER JOHN BARNES PERFORMED A RAP WHICH ENDED,

*"WE'RE **HOWLING** FOR ♬ ENGLAND, ENG-ER-LAND; WE'RE **HOWLING** THE SONG"*

⑥ BOBBY ROBSON'S 1986 WORLD CUP SQUAD BROUGHT THE COUNTRY TO ITS KNEES WITH THEIR SONG,

WE'VE GOT THE WHOLE
♬ *WORLD AT OUR*
HOWLING ♫

⑧ TOP GIRL GROUP THE SPICE GIRLS ADDED THEIR VOICES TO THE 1998 WORLD CUP SONG WHEN THEY SQUAWKED ALONG TO,

♪♫ ***HOWLING***
DOES IT FEEL?

⑦ RON GREENWOOD'S 1982 WORLD CUP SQUAD FAILED TO FULFIL THE PROMISE OF THEIR SONG,

♪ *THIS **HOWLING** WE'LL GET IT RIGHT* ♫

HOWL!

⑨ EVEN FICTIONAL ENGLAND TEAMS HAVE TO MAKE RECORDS THE 2001 FILM *MIKE BASSETT, ENGLAND MANAGER* INCLUDES THE SONG,

♪ *ON ME **HOWLING** SON* ♫

⑩ IT'S WELL KNOWN THAT POP-SINGERS MIME, SO IT'S NO SURPRISE TO DISCOVER THAT FOOTBALLERS DO IT TOO - LIKE DAVID SEAMAN, WHO WAS SO FILLED WITH EMOTION BEFORE THE TEAM'S FIRST GAME IN THE 1990 WORLD CUP THAT HE COULDN'T SING.

*"GOD SAVE THE **HOWLING**"* ♫

Answers:

1 _World Cup Willy_. In case you're wondering, Willy was a cartoon lion used as the mascot for the 1966 tournament.

2 _Back Home_. Amazingly the record, with its promise _We'll fight until the whistle blows, for the folks back home,_ went to No. 1 in the hit parade.

3 _We are the best so forget all the rest_.

4 _Three Lions_.

THE LOUSY LYRICS AWARD...

Three Lions 98 – an "updated" version of the song released to make more money out of the 1998 World Cup. Unfortunately, it included the line, _"Gazza as good as before"_ – which became instantly out of date when Paul "Gazza" Gascoigne was left out of the squad!

5 _"We're playing for England, Eng-er-land; We're playing the song"_. The England fans certainly did play this song. The record went to No. 1 in the charts and stayed there for twelve weeks!

6 _We've Got the Whole World at Our Feet_. Unfortunately, nobody told Argentina this; they knocked England out in the quarter-finals. And the record was even less successful, getting no higher than No. 66 in the charts.

7 *This Time We'll Get it Right.* The record stayed in the charts for ten weeks – which was a lot longer than the team stayed in the tournament!

8 *How Does it Feel?* Pretty awful, in the event. England were knocked out by Argentina on penalties. The only consolation was that the Spice Girls disbanded shortly after making the record.

9 *On Me Head Son.* Unfortunately, the film wasn't a great success. One critic said the fictional England manager was nothing like as funny as some of the real ones!

10 *God Save the Queen.* Yes, Seaman actually mimed singing the National Anthem. To his credit, he made up for it before the Euro 2000 play-off match against Scotland at Hampden Park. The crowd was so noisy that the players couldn't hear the band. When they reached the end of their signing they realized they were ahead of the music – so had to sing the last "God save our Queen" again!

THE REAL-WAY-TO-SING-YOUR-NATIONAL-ANTHEM AWARD...

Hernan Crespo, Argentina – who said before his team played England in the 1998 World Cup finals: "When I sing our national anthem I'll want to eat our rivals alive!".

GLENN'S GLADIATORS (1996–1999)

Glenn Hoddle (1979–1988, 53 caps) had been something of an in-and-out England player: managers put him in against easy teams, then left him out again if the opposition looked tough. So when, after spells in charge of Swindon and Chelsea, he was appointed England manager, gleeful Glenn must have hoped that this time he was in to stay.

At just 39 years old, Hoddle was the youngest-ever England manager. It could be argued that he was also the most imaginative...

Imaginary opponents

During training sessions, the England team would often line up with the ball against – an imaginary team! They would just walk around, without a football, pretending that they were playing a match. The idea was that, by moving around the pitch together, the players would know where they were supposed to be positioned at certain stages of a real game.

HE FOULED ME!

ER...THERE'S NO ONE THERE!

Imaginary selections

Hoddle liked to keep his England team a secret until the last minute, so that opposing managers wouldn't have time to come up with special plans to deal with them. This meant that players he'd picked had to imagine that they weren't playing and not tell anybody that they were!

THE HAS-A-MUM-UNABLE-TO-KEEP-MUM AWARD...

Matthew Le Tissier (1994–97, 8 caps) – who was so excited to be told he was playing at Wembley against Italy in a World Cup qualifier that he couldn't keep quiet about it. He told the good news to his family ... his mum promptly went on the radio and told the whole world!

Imaginary injuries

Another favourite piece of Hoddle hoodwinking was trying to fool the opposing manager by pretending that a particular England player was injured and wouldn't be fit for the match. This really annoyed the newspaper reporters, who found themselves looking stupid when they told their readers about the "injured" player, only to discover that he'd staged a miraculous recovery! Whether the tactic fooled many managers isn't known – but it definitely fooled the footballers. A reporter once asked defender Sol Campbell how his injury was getting on, only to get the reply, "What injury?"

England succeeded in reaching the 1998 World Cup finals in France. The vital qualifying match was the last of all, against Italy, in Rome. England managed the draw they needed with a dogged 0–0 performance.

Much of the excitement was packed into the last two minutes of the match. First England attacked, and striker Ian Wright hit the post. Within seconds, Italy had swept down the pitch and their striker Christian Vieri was jumping for a header ... which went inches wide!

England's regular captain, Alan Shearer, wasn't playing. He was on holiday in Barbados, recovering from a bad injury (a real injury, not an imaginary one!) How did he keep up to date with how the game was going?

a) TV commentary.

b) Telephone commentary.

c) Internet commentary.

Answer: b) He spent 90 minutes on the phone to his dad in Newcastle, listening to Mr Shearer Snr describing the match as he watched it on TV!

Hoddle's healer

The most controversial part of Glenn Hoddle's time as manager was his use of a faith healer. Hoddle believed that certain people had the power to cure illnesses and injuries by touch and prayer. The one he recruited was a lady named Eileen Drewery, and he would suggest to any player with an injury that she might be able to help sort it out...

THE LACK-OF-FAITH-IN-FAITH HEALERS AWARD...

Ray Parlour (1999–2000, 10 caps) – who, when Eileen Drewery laid her hands on his head, asked for a "short back and sides" haircut!

England all-stars: Michael Owen

Michael Owen made his name at the 1998 World Cup. Fancy yourself as another Michael Owen? Then here's what you have to do:

• Aged 8: Begin playing for your Area Primary School's Under-11 team. Michael Owen's team was in Deeside.

• Aged 9: Get yourself made captain.

• Aged 10: Smash a goal-scoring record, preferably one set by a star player. Twenty years before, Ian Rush, later of Liverpool and Wales, had scored 77 goals for the Deeside team. Michael Owen knocked in 92!

He also scored a hat-trick for Liverpool's Youth Team when the won the FA Youth Cup Final against Manchester United; scored on his Liverpool first-team debut against Wimbledon; ended his first full league season as the team's top scorer; came on as substitute in his fourth international against Morocco to become the (then) youngest-ever England goal-scorer.

THE YOU-MUST-BE-JOKING AWARD...

Glenn Hoddle – who, in arguing that Michael Owen didn't yet deserve to be a first-choice for England, said:

He's not a natural goal-scorer.

Owen proved him wrong by scoring one of the World Cup's best-ever goals against Argentina. Here's how to do it in your next school match:

• Get the ball just inside the other team's half.
• Race forward, outpacing the defender who's marking you.
• Go outside another defender who comes to meet you.
• Get inside the penalty area and whack it high into the net!

Oh yes, and while you're at it, win a penalty and score in the penalty shoot-out in the same match!

MISERABLE MATCHES
ENGLAND V ARGENTINA
1998

Michael Owen's contributions turned out to be just about the only bright spots in this World Cup quarter-final. At half-time the score was 2–2. Shortly after, David Beckham was sent off. From then on, England had to defend desperately. At full time the score was still 2–2. Into extra time.

Question: During extra time, Argentina launched an attack when only half the England team were on the pitch. How come?
a) They were getting drinks from the touchline.
b) They didn't realize the second half had started.
c) They were celebrating a goal.

Answer: (c) Defender Sol Campbell thought he'd headed the winner from a corner. Not realizing the referee had disallowed it for a foul on the Argentine goalkeeper, half the team rushed over to congratulate a crazy Campbell.

While they were doing this, the artful Argentines put the ball down and took their free kick! Campbell and the others had to chase back in a hurry. Talk about Sol-destroying!

Even worse was to come. The match ended 2–2 ... and England lost yet another penalty shoot-out. Glenn's gladiators had fought hard, but in the end it was a case of "thumbs down".

The going of Glenn

Hoddle lasted just four games more before a newspaper campaign started to have him removed. What did they say he'd done wrong?

a) Written a diary.

b) Offended disabled people.

c) Lost too many games.

Answer: a) and b) with a little bit of c)

A bad start to their Euro 2000 games gave the newspapers the chance to moan. They hadn't liked the lies Hoddle had told about injured players. When he then brought out a World Cup Diary they suspected he'd not been telling them things because he'd been saving them for his book.

IT SAYS HERE YOU HAD BAKED BEANS FOR BREAKFAST AND YOU SAID IT WAS SPAGHETTI RINGS!

Hoddle was also a believer in reincarnation – that is, that humans live not one life but many lives. When he explained that part of this belief suggested that disabled people could be suffering for wicked things they did in a previous life, the public were outraged. Glenn had to go, the newspapers said, and the FA agreed.

England's record under Glenn Hoddle

Played	Won	Drawn	Lost	Goals For	Goals Ag
28	17	6	5	42	13

ENGLAND FACT FILE

CHAMPIONSHIP PERFORMANCES

In the beginning, friendlies were the most important games England played. Then it became matches in the British Championship. Nowadays, though, it's the games in the European Championship and the World Cup which are the most important. England did well in the friendly games and the British Championship. But what's their record like in the big ones of the World Cup and the Euros? Here are the facts!

WORLD CUP
Qualifying matches
Home: **Played** 40 **Won** 29 **Drawn** 9 **Lost** 2 **Scored** 106 **Let in** 22
Away: **Played** 42 **Won** 24 **Drawn** 10 **Lost** 8 **Scored** 86 **Let in** 32

TOTALS Played 82 **Won** 53 **Drawn** 19 **Lost** 10 **Scored** 192 **Let in** 54

Finals tournaments
TOTALS Played 50 **Won** 22 **Drawn** 15 **Lost** 13 **Scored** 68 **Let in** 45

EUROPEAN CHAMPIONSHIPS (up to and including Euro 2004 finals)

Qualifying matches
Home: **Played** 35 **Won** 23 **Drawn** 8 **Lost** 4 **Scored** 83 **Let in** 16
Away: **Played** 35 **Won** 21 **Drawn** 11 **Lost** 3 **Scored** 66 **Let in** 27

TOTALS Played 70 **Won** 44 **Drawn** 19 **Lost** 7 **Scored** 149 **Let in** 43

Finals tournaments
TOTALS Played 23 **Won** 7 **Drawn** 7 **Lost** 9 **Scored** 31 **Let in** 28

THE FOUL ENGLAND QUIZ

Football can be foul – and international football can be even fouler! When Huddersfield Town and England centre half Alf Young (1932–1938, 9 caps) first faced the up-and-coming Tommy Lawton (1938–48, 23 caps) in a league match, he gave him the stern warning:

Thee can go past me, and the ball can go past – but thee and the ball are not going past together!

Try this quiz about injuries sustained by various England players. You're given the details but, just as 'ard Alf was threatening to do to trembling Tommy, we've jumbled up the parts of the body. Sort them out so that the right body part goes with the right fact.

---

1 In the build-up to the annual battle against Scotland in 1948, an excited newspaper report said that leaping Tommy Lawton was in doubt and receiving treatment for a <u>back</u> injury – when in fact he'd only grazed it and dabbed disinfectant on it!

2 When this match was eventually played, England's goalkeeper Frank Swift (1946–1949, 19 caps), was flattened. He recovered, to play on with two broken <u>eyes</u>.

3 In 1964, midfielder Alan Mullery was forced to miss England's summer tour to Dublin and New York after he'd strained his <u>cheek</u> while shaving.

---

4 Action-man Bryan Robson lasted just over 30 minutes of England's 1986 World Cup match against Morocco before walking painfully off the field with a dislocated <u>knee</u>.

5 Stanley Matthews confessed that he suffered with an upset <u>shoulder</u> before every big match he played.

6 After a violent game against Italy in 1934, midfield man Eddie Hapgood (1933–1939, 30 caps) said, "It's a bit hard to play like a gentleman when somebody closely resembling an enthusiastic member of the Mafia is wiping his studs down your <u>whole body</u>".

7 Another match against Italy, this time in 1948, saw history made as Jack Howe (1948–1949, 3 caps) became the first England player to perform wearing devices to help with his defective <u>teeth</u>.

8 When centre forward Tommy Taylor (1953–1957, 19 caps) scored for England against the Republic of Ireland in 1957, his teammate Frank Blunstone got so excited he knocked out his own <u>stomach</u>.

9 In 1951, during a 2–3 defeat by Scotland, England forward Wilf Mannion (1946–1951, 26 caps) was left speechless after fracturing his <u>ribs</u>.

10 None of these injuries come close to what nearly happened to forward Stan Mortensen (1947–1953, 25 caps) before the 1950 World Cup in Brazil ever got under way. He was out walking and almost injured his <u>legs</u>.

Answers:

1 Knee. Lawton played and England won 2–0.

2 Ribs. The injury was only discovered after Swift had collapsed on a Manchester railway train – and a quick-thinking porter wheeled him away on his trolley!

3 Back. Mrs Mullery explained: "He turned round to pick up his shaving brush and his legs gave way." It's not known if she was bristling with anger!

THE PUT-YOUR-BACK-IN-TO-IT AWARD...

Les Cocker – England trainer for the 1970 World Cup with Alf Ramsey. During the tournament, Ramsey's attention to detail made sure the players stayed injury-free. The only casualty was Cocker, who had to spend two days in bed after straining his back trying to lift one of the team's bulging kitbags!

4 Shoulder. Robson did this four times all told. He also collected three broken legs, two broken noses, a broken finger, two torn hamstrings, torn ankle ligaments, two doses of concussion and enough bruised bones to make anybody feel blue ... and still won 90 caps! England manager Bobby Robson reckoned that his injuries stopped him winning another 30. Not bad for a player who wasn't picked for his county as a schoolboy!

5 Stomach. Matthews was always sick before a big game. As he played his final serious game after getting a knee injury at the age of 70, that's a lot of sick!

6 Legs. The match, which England won 3–2, was known from then on as "The Battle of Highbury" after the ground where it was played.

7 Eyes. Howe was the first England international to wear contact lenses.

THE SHINING-PERFORMANCE AWARD...

Ted Ditchburn (1948–1956, 6 caps). In 1949, and playing only his second international, Ditchburn let in three first-half goals against Sweden. He claimed he'd been blinded by the sun. He kept a clean sheet in the second half but England still lost the match 1–3.

8 Teeth ... to be exact, the false teeth he wore when he wasn't playing – because he wasn't. Blunstone was a reserve, watching in the stands, and his teeth shot out when he leapt to his feet in excitement!

9 Cheek. Amazingly, the person who left the match to accompany Mannion to hospital was the England manager Walter Winterbottom.

10 Whole body … or perhaps that should be "hole" body. Mortensen was out walking in Rio de Janeiro and fell down a hole left by workers who'd just removed a tree.

KEVIN'S KREW (1999–2000)

Do you remember Kevin Keegan – he of the shorts round his ankles in Alf Ramsey's time? To a fortune teller, that incident would have predicted Keegan's life as England's next manager ... because his time in the job was short, and under him the team's performances were mostly down.

I SEE A TEAM IN BOTTOM PLACE...

As a player, Keegan won lots of trophies with Liverpool. After a time with German club Hamburg, cracker Kevin returned to play for Southampton and Newcastle, where his sparkling performances made him a tremendously popular figure. He later became Newcastle's manager, then did the same job at Fulham.

Keeganisms

Both as a manager and a TV pundit, Keegan's tongue seemed to be as non-stop a performer as his feet used to be. Unfortunately, it wasn't as skilful. Even before he was appointed, clumsy Kevin had a huge collection of daft quotes to his name...

- "That decision, for me, was almost certainly definitely wrong."
- "It's like a toaster, the ref's shirt pocket. Every time there's a tackle, up pops a yellow card."

- "A tremendous strike which hit the defender full on the arm – and it nearly came off."
- "He's using his strength and that is his strength, his strength."
- "Goalkeepers aren't born today until they're in their late twenties or thirties and sometimes not even then."

… and to everybody's delight, they didn't stop once he was England manager!

- *Before England met Scotland in a play-off to decide which of the two countries would compete in the Euro 2000 finals:* "England have the best fans in the world and Scotland's fans are second-to-none."
- *Setting realistic performance targets:* I want more from David Beckham. "I want him to improve on perfection."
- *Making results look good:* "You can't do better than go away from home and get a draw."
- *Showing an appreciation of football history:* "England can end the millennium as it started – as the greatest football nation in the world."
- *Not falling into the Glenn Hoddle trap of lying about injuries:* "There's a slight doubt about only one player, and that's Tony Adams, who won't be playing tomorrow."

England all-star: Paul Scholes

At his club, Manchester United, red-haired Paul Scholes (1997–2004, 66 caps) was nicknamed "The Ginger Prince". As for the United fans, their regular chant about the player was: "Paul Scholes, he scores goals!"

That was certainly true in the first match played by Keegan's England, a European Championship qualifier against Poland. England won 3–1, with all three goals from Scholes.

Unfortunately, two matches later, in another Euro-game against Sweden, manager and player didn't seem to be speaking the same language. Before the match Keegan instructed Scholes to "drop little bombs all over the pitch" – meaning, give the other team surprises. In the end it was poor Paul who got the surprise: he was sent off after committing two bad fouls and the game ended 0–0.

It all came good again though, as Scholes hit both England's goals in a play-off game against Scotland to send England to Euro 2000 … where, after only three minutes of their first match against Portugal, it was a case of goals-happy to Scholes-happy as he scored another one.

Sadly, that was that. From 2–0 up, England lost 2–3 and eventually went out of the tournament after failing to qualify from their group.

THE INTERESTING–INTERNATIONAL–DEBUT AWARD…

Richard Wright (2000–2001, 2 caps) who, picked by Keegan to play his first match for England against Malta, gave away a penalty after 29 minutes; had the penalty kick count as an own-goal when it bounced off him and dribbled into the net; then saved a second penalty two minutes before the end to deny Malta an equalizer!

MISERABLE MATCHES
ENGLAND V GERMANY
2000

England's one high-spot at Euro 2000 had been in beating Germany, 1–0. Just four months later the two teams were meeting again, this time in a World Cup qualifying match.

Question: The game was a famous "last". What was it?

a) Alan Shearer's last match as England captain.

b) The last match played at Wembley stadium.

c) Kevin Keegan's last match as England manager.

Answer: b) and c) Wembley was being knocked down to make way for a new stadium, so this one was meant to be a celebration! It wasn't. England lost 1–0 and Kevin Keegan didn't even wait for the players to come out of the shower before telling them he was resigning.

He then told the rest of the world why he didn't want to carry on doing the job.

> *It's a massive job. Lots of the parts I did very well, but not the key part of getting players to win football matches.*

England's record under Kevin Keegan

For once, Keegan never spoke a truer word. England's record during his time in office was the worst of any manager.

Played	Won	Drawn	Lost	Goals For	Goals Ag
18	7	7	4	26	15

A couple of caretakers

After Glenn Hoddle's sudden departure, Howard Wilkinson – manager of Leeds United for eight years before he was sacked – had taken charge for one match, a friendly against France. Wilkinson now stood in for another match, a European qualifier against Finland. This time he did better – the team drew 0–0!

And that was the end of wobbly Wilkinson, the first England manager never to win a game while he was in charge.

England's record under Howard Wilkinson

Played	Won	Drawn	Lost	Goals For	Goals Ag
2	0	1	1	0	2

Wilkinson was followed as caretaker manager by Peter Taylor. He was in charge for just one match, a friendly against Italy. In a bold move, he made David Beckham captain. England still lost 1–0, though, and that was the end of tottering Taylor – the second England manager never to win a game while he was in charge!

England's record under Peter Taylor

Played	Won	Drawn	Lost	Goals For	Goals Ag
1	0	0	1	0	1

The FA had decided that neither Wilkinson nor Taylor was good enough to keep the job of England manager permanently.

The question was – who in England did they think was good enough? The answer to that was … nobody.

ENGLAND FACT FILE

SCORCHING SKIPPERS

Peter Taylor did one important thing in his sole match in charge – he appointed David Beckham as the 103rd captain in England's history. But where does David Beckham stand in the list of all-time captains? And how successful has he been compared to all the others? Here are the crucial captaincy facts!

Caps as captain
1 Billy Wright (1948–1959) 90 times in 105 games
1 Bobby Moore (1963–1973) 90 times in 108 games
3 Bryan Robson (1982–1991) 65 times in 90 games
4 David Beckham (2000–present) 50 times in 86 games
5 Alan Shearer (1996–2000) 34 times in 63 games

Team wins as captain
1 Bobby Moore (57 wins out of 90) 63
2 David Beckham (28 wins out of 50) 56
3 Billy Wright (49 wins out of 90) 54
4 Bryan Robson (32 wins out of 65) 49
5 Alan Shearer (16 wins out of 34) 47

But none of these match the record of a scorching skipper from the distant past Vivian Woodward (1908–1911) (12 wins out of 14) 86

Although if vibrant Viv had played as many games as the other captains, perhaps his record wood-n't have been so good!

SVEN'S MEN (2000–2006)

The manager England found next wasn't English. Or Irish, or Welsh. He wasn't even Scottish. In fact, he wasn't British at all. He was Swedish. His name: Sven-Goran Eriksson.

Energetic Eriksson had spent his playing days charging around as a full-back in the lower divisions of the Swedish league until a knee injury had forced him to retire. That's when he'd taken up coaching – very successfully. He'd gone on to win trophies managing clubs in Sweden, Portugal and Italy.

Words of welcome

Enthusiastic Eriksson explained why he'd accepted the job. Said Sven:

> *You can't say no when you have been offered the manager of England. It is so big.*

Having a non-English manager of England caused a lot of argument. Some people were very upset, like journalist Jeff Powell of the *Daily Mail* (the man who wrote Bobby Moore's biography):

> *So, the mother country of football, birthplace of the greatest game, has finally gone from the cradle to the shame. We've sold our birthright down the fjord to a nation of seven million skiers and hammer throwers who spend half their lives in darkness.*

Some people though, like ex-Nottingham Forest and Derby County manager Brian Clough saw the advantages:

> *At last England have appointed a manager who speaks English better than the players.*

THE I-CAN-READ-AS-WELL-AS TALK AWARD...

Sven-Goran Eriksson – who also said, "I have read that all [England managers] have been declared idiots at some time in their career, so I know what to expect."

Eriksson's England faced their first big test when they travelled to Germany for a World Cup 2002 qualifying match. Germany were confident. "We are as good, if not better than, Eriksson's side – we will win," said ex-German captain Franz Beckenbauer. And it certainly looked as if Germany would win as they went into a 1–0 lead through their towering striker, Carsten Jancker – who himself had said before the match...

> *We don't have to worry about Michael Owen. We have a stronger team and that is what counts.*

Carsten should have been more cautious. It was Michael Owen who hit an equalizer for England. Then, just before half-time, Steven Gerrard scored to put England 2–1 ahead, embarrassing another of Germany's players' Steffen Effenberg, who'd sneered before the match:

> *Steven who? I don't know him. I am not interested in England, or who is in their squad. I don't have time. I have better things to do.*

In the second half, England roared on. Owen scored two more goals to complete his hat-trick and Emile Heskey added another to give England an historic 5–1 victory. Exactly how historic? Ask ex-Germany international Uli Hoeness, who said before the game:

> *How are England going to win in Germany? It hasn't happened for 100 years!*

Unfortunately it's getting to be nearly that long since England have won the World Cup itself. After going on to qualify for the 2002 competition in Korea and Japan, they were knocked out in the quarter-finals by Brazil.

England all-star: David Beckham

Since his debut against Moldova in 1996, David Beckham had undoubtedly become a vital part of the England team. As another German player, Sebastian Dreisler, had sneered before England's epic 5–1 victory in 2001:

> *I am glad that David Beckham will be fit. Now England will have no excuses when we beat them.*

Beckham's trademark is his bending free kick – and his most important Sven-bend happened right at the end of the World Cup qualifying match against

Greece in October 2001. With just a few minutes left, and England needing a goal to qualify automatically for the finals, up stepped Beckham.

Want to try what he did yourself? Here's how – as described by research workers of Yamagata University in Japan and the UK's University of Sheffield:

① USING THE INSTEP OF YOUR RIGHT FOOT, STRIKE THE BALL 8 CENTIMETRES TO THE RIGHT OF ITS CENTRE...

② MAKING IT ACCELERATE TO 80 MILES AN HOUR...

③ WHILE SPINNING ANTICLOCKWISE AT 8 REVOLUTIONS PER SECOND

④ THIS SHOULD MAKE THE BALL SHOOT INTO THE AIR AS IF SOARING OVER THE GOALS CROSSBAR...

⑤ THEN SLOW TO 40 MILES AN HOUR...

⑥ AS IT CURVES FURTHER TO THE LEFT...

⑦ AND DROPS INTO THE TOP CORNER OF THE GOAL!

IMPORTANT POINT: You must kick it in the right direction. Aim it the wrong way and you'll score the most beautiful own-goal in the history of football!

Submerged by subs

Not many countries have provoked rule changes, but
England have managed it. When England played
Australia on 12 February 2003, some of the players
were substituted for the second half. How many?
a) 1–5 **b)** 6–9 **c)** 9–11

Answer: c) The maximum, 11. Yes, a completely
different England team came out for the second
half. If they'd all been amateurs you could have
been forgiven for thinking we were back in 1891!

The following year the international Football
Association, FIFA, brought in a new rule saying that
no more than six substitutes could be used during a
friendly international match.

England all-star: Wayne Rooney

One of Eriksson's record eleven second-half substitutes for that match against Australia was making a record of his own. When he ran out as the 1,125th player to appear for England, he also became the youngest – at 17 years 111 days.

By the time the 2004–2005 season ended, wonderkid Wayne had earned 23 caps ... but hadn't played a whole match! He'd come on as a substitute in three of them, and been substituted himself in the other 20!

He'd made his mark while he had been on the pitch, though. In Euro 2004, in Portugal, he was England's top scorer, with four goals. Sven was delighted with him, the England fans were delighted with him ... but most delighted of all were the newspaper headline writers! Here's what they had to say after Rooney's couple of goals against Croatia put England into the quarter-finals:

Why not try making up some headlines of your own? But make sure you use scrap paper. You don't want to get into trouble for roo-ining your school books!

MISERABLE MATCHES
PORTUGAL V ENGLAND
2004

It's said that history repeats itself. That certainly seemed true for England in this game. Here's what happened...

European Championships, 2004
Portugal v. England World Cup, 1998
Argentina v. England

- England go ahead (1–0) through a goal by Michael Owen...
- England go ahead (2–1) through a goal by Michael Owen...
- England lose a player – Wayne Rooney – with an injured foot...
- England lose a player – David Beckham, who is sent off for using his foot to foul Argentina's Diego Simeone ...
- The teams are level at full time (1–1)...
- The teams are level at full time (2–2)...
- In extra time, England have a goal disallowed – "scored" by defender Sol Campbell...
- In extra time, England have a goal disallowed – "scored" by defender Sol Campbell...
- At the end of extra time the scores are level at 2–2...
- At the end of extra time the scores are level at 2–2...
- England lose the penalty shoot-out!
- England lose the penalty shoot-out!

After the game was over, Wayne Rooney was found to have broken one of the five long bones in his foot

158

called the metatarsals. It was another case of history repeating itself. Back in 2002, England players David Beckham and Gary Neville had both suffered the same injury!

I'VE BROKE THE METER ... THE MATER ... THE MOTAR ... I'VE BROKE THE BONE WHAT LEADS FROM ME SHIN TO ME PINKIE, RIGHT?

The question is, will history continue to repeat itself for Sven's men? Like ... a repeat of 1966 and another World Cup win one day? Sven Goran-Eriksson only has one more chance. He'll be leaving his job after the 2006 World Cup.

England's record under Sven-Goran Eriksson – so far...

Played	Won	Drawn	Lost	Goals For	Goals Ag
58	33	15	10	108	55

ENGLAND FACT FILE

MASTERFUL MANAGERS

It's the players who win the matches for England, of course, but it's the manager who picks them. So – who's managed to be the most perfect picker in England's long history? Here are the masterful facts!

1 Alf Ramsey 61.1 (69 wins in 113 games)
1 FA Selection Committee 61.1 (138 wins in 226 games)
3 Glenn Hoddle 60.7 (17 wins in 28 games)
4 Ron Greenwood 60.0 (33 wins in 55 games)
5 Sven-Goran Eriksson 56.8 (33 wins in 58 games)
6 Walter Winterbottom 56.1 (78 wins in 139 games)
7 Bobby Robson 49.5 (47 wins in 95 games)
8 Don Revie 48.2 (14 wins in 29 games)
9 Terry Venables 47.8 (11 wins in 23 games)
10 Graham Taylor 47.4 (18 wins in 38 games)
11 Joe Mercer 42.9 (3 wins in 7 games)
12 Kevin Keegan 38.9 (7 wins in 18 games)

Perhaps England should go back to having a selection committee to pick their team! One thing's for sure, though. Whoever's in charge, England will still have a team to cheer for and players itching to be picked for them.

Perhaps one day you'll be one of those players. Maybe it will be you the spectators are cheering for as you represent your country. Why not? It's certainly an ambition worth aiming for. Ask ex-England striker, Gary Lineker. He always said:

It's the biggest thrill to pull on the white shirt and walk out with the England team.